Pastures of Healing

Denis Glennon AO

One of seventy-plus million Irish diaspora scattered around the planet, Denis made Western Australia his new home in 1974. He spent over forty years in the corporate world, in various parts of the globe.

In 1997, his life was shattered when his daughter Ciara was murdered.

Drawing on inner and outer strengths, he has dealt with the intense grief of Ciara's murder.

His book, *Pastures of Healing*, is an uplifting narrative, depicting the pathways he discovered and journeyed and the manifestations he experienced, to return himself, and assist his family's return, to the world of the living.

His wife, Una, has written of her own grief of losing Ciara in her book *Ciara's Gift: Grief Edged with Gold.*

Late afternoon light reflects off a sandbar in the salt flats, just south of Penong, on the South Australian coast, outlining an unknown artist's hand, the symbolic drip of paint defining the edge of the land we live in.

Cover image used with the permission of Tony Hewitt, captured during *Girt by Sea*, an aerial photography circumnavigation of Australia undertaken by photographers Denis Glennon and Tony Hewitt.

Denis Glennon

Pastures of Healing

from the loss of a child

First published in Australia in 2023
by Upswell Publishing
Perth, Western Australia
upswellpublishing.com

This book is copyright. Apart from any fair dealing for the purpose of private study, research, criticism or review, as permitted under the *Copyright Act 1968*, no part may be reproduced by any process without written permission. Enquiries should be made to the publisher.

Copyright © 2023 by Denis Glennon

The moral right of the author has been asserted.

ISBN: 978-0-645-53682-9

A catalogue record for this book is available from the National Library of Australia

Cover design by Chil3, Fremantle
Typeset in Foundry Origin by Lasertype
Printed in China by 1010 Printing

Upswell Publishing is assisted by the State of Western Australia through its funding program for arts and culture.

To

My daughter *Ciara*

The two strong women who stood by me, through everything, *Una and Denise*.

Thank you both, sincerely.

My four grandchildren: *Ailish, Toby, Liam and Angus*. Be kind to each other and take care of one another.

The remarkable people of Western Australia, who supported us for so long.

The Claddagh design has significance for my family.
The Claddagh brooch Ciara was wearing at the
time of her murder has never been found.

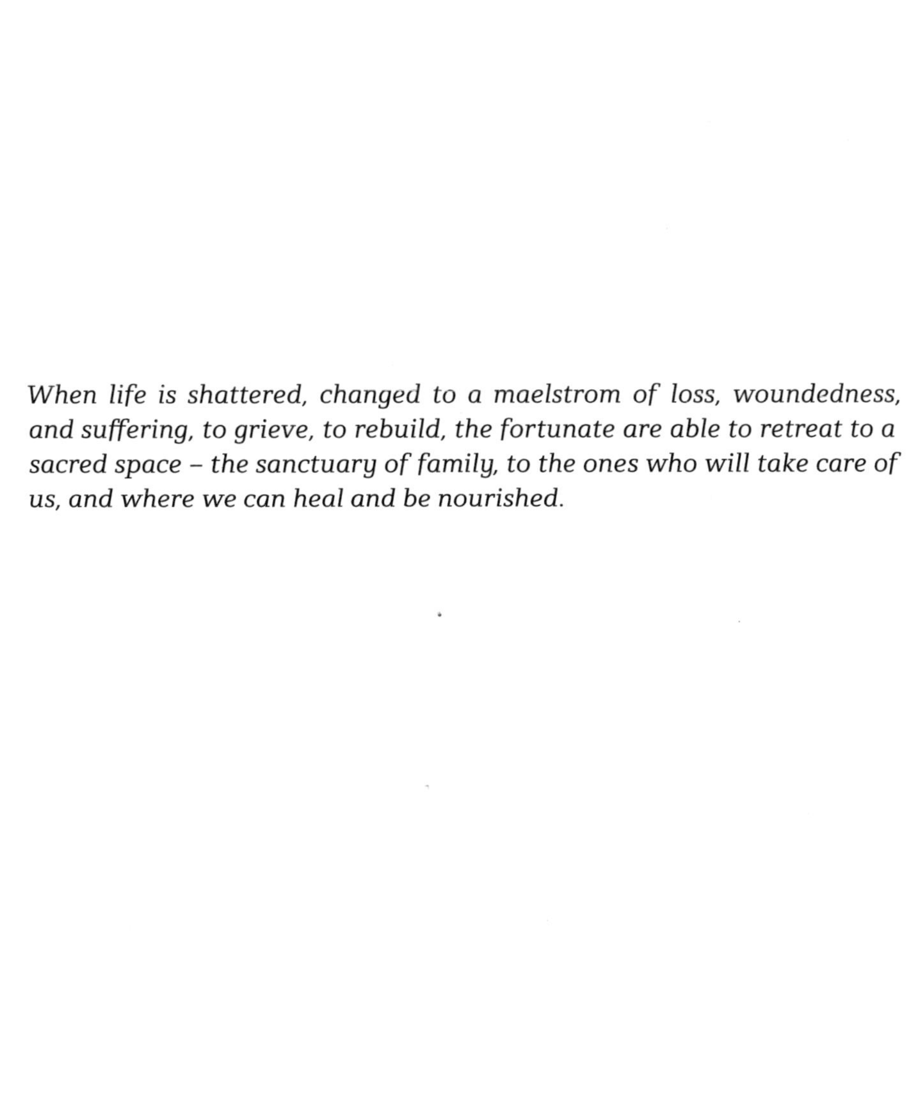

When life is shattered, changed to a maelstrom of loss, woundedness, and suffering, to grieve, to rebuild, the fortunate are able to retreat to a sacred space – the sanctuary of family, to the ones who will take care of us, and where we can heal and be nourished.

Author's Statement

The content of this book has been influenced by my lived experience of the murder of our daughter Ciara; attendances at many presentations and talks by my wife, Una Glennon; her book, *Ciara's Gift: Grief Edged with Gold*; notes I wrote for my own presentations and talks; personal media statements; and many resources, books and articles, the vast majority of which are listed in the Bibliography.

I searched and read intermittently over a period of twenty-five years.

Along the way, especially in the earlier years, I made short handwritten notes which I retained and re-read many times, for help. The sources I visited in the early years were not referenced in my handwritten notes. I have no way of tracing or checking references for the material that found its way into the handwritten notes I made fifteen to twenty years ago.

At that time, I did not envisage writing this book.

Only once I contemplated writing the book did I commence a formal recording of sources and references. I have made every effort to recognise the work of others I have visited, and I list these in the Bibliography.

If you recognise a piece of your writing in the book, please consider it as an acknowledgement of a source of help onto which I grasped, with gratitude, at the time I read it and wrote it down, to revisit and help uplift me at low points.

I welcome any copyright holders who have not been traced and are not mentioned in the Bibliography to contact me.

In this book the text that appears in bold in quoted material shows my own emphasis.

Contents

Foreword

As the author Denis Glennon writes and as all parents who have suffered the loss of a child know painfully and uninvitedly too well, the raw truth is that sometimes terrible things happen in this life. It was in the depth of a then-unsolved tragedy that Denis and I were brought together. He as a grieving father and husband and I as a senior police officer in the Western Australia Police Force. Ciara Glennon, Denis and Una's daughter, a twenty-seven year old best friend and sister to Denise, had been abducted and murdered.

Two other young women had earlier been abducted and murdered and the people of Western Australia were in shock, appalled and outraged at the innocent loss of life to such horrific crimes.

Over the following twenty years Denis and I came to know, understand and implicitly trust each other. We had to. Our united goal was to find the person responsible for Ciara's murder. That goal was shared by over five hundred dedicated police officers, analysts, profilers, scientists and later, prosecutors. I posit that all West Australians, bar the murderer, earnestly yearned for justice.

A great injustice was tearing at every part of Denis. His body, mind, heart and spirit.

In the anguished pit of grief, Denis describes how his determination to survive this unfathomable loss forced him to search for meaning, a way out of that pit that defied conventional processes and stages of grief, forgiveness and that oft-used misnomer, closure. His journey to reach a state of contentment was punctuated by doubts, anger and frustration at God, at humanity, at the lack of understanding of the crime and initial absence of strength to carry on, all while striving to take care of his family, each on their own journey of grief.

The impact of this book will reverberate beyond the parents who have suffered from the loss of a child to a much wider readership including, clinicians, counsellors, family and friends of affected persons and practitioners from all walks of life.

You will find this book deeply moving and of undoubted comfort. You will also find the Denis I know. A man of dignity, strength and grace in the face of unspeakable horror. A man of wisdom, intellect, courage, unwavering determination, love, spirituality and honesty. He takes you deep into his private spaces and reveals the only ones who entirely understand grief are those who have lived through it. Denis shows his innermost drivers and shines hope for those in mourning as he progresses from inaction to action, from despair to hope and ultimately, contentment in the life he now lives.

The Hon. Chris Dawson AC, APM
Governor of Western Australia
January 2023

Acknowledgements

I acknowledge, with gratitude, the extraordinary debt I owe to many people whose steadfast presence sustained me and made this book possible. In particular, I thank Una – the lady to whom I retreated, who took care of me and whose comments on my early scribblings were exceptionally helpful.

Denise, Ailish, Toby, Liam and Angus – we have had a tough run but how tall you all stand.

His Excellency the Honourable Christopher John Dawson AC, APM, Governor of Western Australia for writing the very thoughtful Foreword.

The late Sister Carmel who came to just sit with me, at home, when the world shattered beneath me. Your sacred, silent presence was sufficient; no words were needed. The Presentations Sisters at Iona College, Mosman Park opened their chapel to us; I will be forever grateful for its safe retreat.

I thank business colleagues and friends who remained steadfast and solid, a number of whom have sadly passed away - the Board members of the Secure Community Foundation, (who arranged substantial initial funding to secure innovative analytical DNA technology for Western Australia), the late Terry O'Connor QC, (who provided early sanctuary for my family to absorb the initial horror of Ciara's murder), Dennis O'Neil, (a stalwart, fellow Board Member and good friend), Julie Bishop, (a friend, who always provided support, in so many ways), Lorna Forster, (the most generous and caring Executive Assistant), John Carrington, Adrian Chai and colleagues at Ashurst, (colleagues at Ciara's place of employment), the late Fr Joe Walsh, (the most considerate priest I ever knew), good friends Neil Fearis, Geoff Totterdell, Keith Jones, and Craig Carter, (men I could depend on, when needed), Dr Chris Whittaker, Dr Paul Vogel and Dr Rod Lukatelich, (colleagues who understood), African colleagues Shem Compion and André Cloete (who accompanied me into the African bush, where I experienced peace-filled moments), the numerous Vice Chancellors, Deans of the University of Western Australia (UWA) Law School, Professors Robyn Carroll and Meredith Blake and law school staff associated with the scholarship established in Ciara's memory.

My long standing and loyal friends, Jim and the late Lis McIntyre.

Tom and Bernadette Glennon, Dermot and Margaret Glennon, and their families; Padraig Mooney and the late Cora Mooney, Moy and Gerry Murphy, the late Donal and Maeve Mooney, and their families; thank you for being always there and especially when I re-visited Ireland in those dark days.

Photographer and friend, Tony Hewitt, thank you for permission to use your image for the jacket cover and Becky Chilcot for the cover design.

Former WA Police Commissioner, Chris Dawson, and former Deputy Commissioner Stephen Brown, thank you for ensuring the necessary resources were allocated to the lengthy investigation, for nearly a quarter of a century. To the many WA police officers, investigators and PathWest scientists for their endless work, professionalism, perseverance, and resilience over twenty plus years; my sincere thanks.

I extend a very special thanks to Carmel Barbagallo SC, Office of the Director of Public Prosecutions for Western Australia, now a Judge of the District Court of Western Australia, and her team at ODPP – my family will forever be in your debt.

The initial thoughts of writing this book were unsettling. From where within me could I mine thirty-five to forty thousand words? Terri-ann White, ex-Director of UWA Publishing, now Director of Upswell Publishing, has been associated with my family since the publication of Una's book: *Ciara's Gift – grief edged with gold*, in 2012. She encouraged and supported every step of the process from conception to publication, was gracious in reviewing my early rambling drafts, offering insights, warnings, and silence at the right times.

Thank you, Editor Kelly Somers; without losing anything important, you transformed the too-wordy draft into a book.

PART I

1
Introduction

Everyone can master grief but he that has it.

William Shakespeare

Unless a parent has experienced the woundedness, suffering and grief that accompany the loss of their child, they cannot truly know its startling impacts on body, mind, heart and spirit.

There is no abacus for this kind of grief.

Only by its diminishment, not absence, is progress measured.

The early days cascade over one another, bringing with them a foreboding, formless darkness, a fog of physical and emotional fatigue, a heartless isolation in a forced, altered world. No parent who has lost a child can escape this new world.

It is a stony world, sculpted by the razor-sharp chisel of uninvited grief.

Parents must somehow maintain a mindset of silent defiance whilst they search for pathways to strengthen their instincts to survive. For this to happen, new mental toughness, new courage and new wisdom must be found so they can summon effort into every day and every step forward. Otherwise, they may remain numbed, deadened, by their grief, for a long time, perhaps forever.

I was one of the fortunate ones. I found restored strength, courage, pathways, teachings, enlightenments and awakened understandings to rebuild life. Some of these transpired only in times of surrender, letting the mystery of healing manifest.

Buddhist monk Thich Nhat Hanh in his book *No Death, No Fear* stated: *We can only accept teachings that we have put into practice with our own awakened understanding and that we can see with our own experience to be true.*

Whilst writing, I have tried to stay with this principle.

I hope each time this book is read, it offers a little strength, courage and help to all parents carrying the burden of the excruciating grief from the loss of their child.

We can repair our cracks, grow again, becoming different people who are content with their new self and who are more resilient and stronger.

2
Definitions

Please take a moment to read this chapter as I use a small number of terms repeatedly throughout the book. The meanings I give to the terms are personal but will help you understand how I found healings that underpinned the diminishment of my grief.

The terms *pain, woundedness, suffering, grief* and *deep grief* are used interchangeably in the literature on grief. The term *manifestation* has different meanings, dependent on the context in which it is used.

In this book I define these terms as follows:

Pain

This is the feeling or sensation we experience when we injure a part of our body.

Pain manifests itself from injuries such as a deep knife cut to a finger, dislocation of a shoulder, a broken leg, a back injury from a herniated disc or fractured vertebrae. *Pain* is the unpleasant experience which affects our *body*, at a physical level. This *pain* will repair, will heal. External signs of the injury will most likely disappear; there are no long-lasting feelings of physical, psychological, emotional or spiritual hurt. We return to normal life; we forget the early *pain*. With the assistance of medical attention and time to heal, we recover to be the person we were before the injury.

Woundedness

Woundedness is a form of permanent harm or hurt to our body, mind, emotions or spirit, which changes us, forever. Examples of *woundedness* are the amputation of an arm or leg; severe loss of hearing in both ears; monoplegia and hemiplegia – forms of paralysis resulting from a stroke.

The amputated arm or leg will never regrow. The lost hearing will never return. Currently, there is no cure for paralysis. The *woundedness* becomes a permanent part of us. We will not return to be the same person again. We become an *altered* person.

The loss of a child results in *woundedness*, for all parents.

This form of *woundedness* is never fully fixed, cured, nor forgotten; its ability to continue to inflict hurt diminishes, but never goes away.

Whilst experiencing *woundedness*, we may appear externally to be fully functional, but the loss cannot be remedied.

We have two broad choices to deal with it:

> accept the *woundedness* is now part of who we have become, seek pathways to diminish its impacts, and learn how we can live with it, or

> not accept it will be part of us forever, refute its presence, try avoiding it, fight against it, and continue to experience *suffering* for years, perhaps for the rest of our lives.

These two choices are eloquently summarised by Holocaust survivor Victor Frankl in his book, *Man's Search for Meaning*, where he quotes the Russian novelist Fyodor Dostoevsky:

> *There is only one thing that I dread: not to be worthy of my sufferings. Our sufferings can be either obstacles or opportunities. The only difference is how we view them. Our experiences can be either stumbling blocks or steppingstones on the path of life.* ***The difference is how we use them.*** *It is not our circumstances but* how we react to them *that matters. It is not what happens to us, but* **what we do with what happens that matters** *the most in life.*

I concur with this view.

Our diminishment of grief is contingent on what actions we take, what we do, along the way.

Suffering

Suffering is what we experience, when we intentionally do not accept that our *woundedness* has become a permanent part of who we have become; we do not find pathways to fit our *woundedness* into our altered life, to learn to live with the *woundedness*. There is no such thing as a full recovery from the grief of losing our child, as we would experience from mere *pain*. We emerge as *altered* people.

Suffering happens to persons, not to bodies.

Grief and Deep Grief

Nicholas Wolterstorff lost his son in a mountaineering accident. In his book, *Lament for a Son*, he says: *Grief is a special kind of suffering. It is intensely wanting what you know cannot be.*

I agree with him.

I experienced similar *grief* as I searched for pathways towards an acceptance of my *woundedness*, as I learned to *live with* my grief, to *incorporate, integrate* it into my *altered* life and self.

I write about *grief* from this lived experience.

Grief becomes *deep grief* when *suffering* continues and continues; the *wounded* person sees no way through the shadowland of their *grief,* just helplessness, not knowing if they will survive.

This kind of grief is a complex mix of physical vulnerabilities, cognitive incongruity, emotional hurts and spiritual doubts, over which we believe we have no control – a mutation of our feelings compressed into a churning cauldron of sadness, with no endpoint visible.

Such *deep grief* can change us forever, always for the worse.

Fortunately, I did not suffer *deep grief*, as I define it here.

Manifestation

The definition I use originates in the late Latin noun, *manifestatio*, and the verb *manifestare*, to 'make public' (to yourself and/or to others).

Manifestation is what takes place when an insight or revelation I experience is turned into a reality, by what I do, by the action I take.

The insight or revelation alone is but the transitory light bulb thought or moment that may ignite an intent to do something. Too many times I mistook intent for action.

Our intent can be so good that we can't conceive that it is not actually manifesting itself in a particular situation. Recognition of the signs of this falsity is frequently murky.

What I do with my interpretation of the insight or revelation, the action I initiate to turn my intent into a reality, is what matters.

Manifestation is the process of taking an insight, a revelation and initiating the necessary action to make the intent a reality.

This conversion to a reality is possible for all parents if they are willing to put in the work, to initiate action. This is where the power of *manifestation* resides, waiting to be mined, revealing golden nuggets of understanding and especially of healing of grief.

Manifestation always involves the breaking of new ground, the crossing of a threshold, from a comfortable mind place to an uncomfortable, unknown mind place. It requires taking a risk and trusting in one's own ability to make the crossing and deal with whatever is found on the other side.

Whilst manifestation can be an intimidating concept and process, its potency to heal grief is immeasurable.

There is something buried in all of us that contrives to keep us within safe borders, to remain where we are, to not take risks, to not take unlit pathways that invite us to cross thresholds to unknown destinations.

We prefer to remain within our ruminations, though they be grief filled. We are content to read more, analyse more, even continue to wallow around in misery. Anything to avert initiating the necessary action.

When we do initiate action, we are manifesting it, making it public, not only to ourselves but also to family members, friends, colleagues and members of our broader community who recognise this commitment. Committing publicly, no matter how miniscule it may seem, imbues in us a sense of responsibility, an obligation to see things through. It strengthens our self-respect, our confidence and resilience, to find pathways to healing of our grief.

I know from hard-won experience that hesitancy and indecision claimed my mind for prolonged periods before I initiated the necessary action at the times I received insights and revelations. Occasionally, a time for grounding was required, during which the fleeting revelation developed and honed itself into an acute clarity.

Yet I needlessly delayed and beat around the bush when I should simply have taken the risk and trusted to initiate action when a pathway to healing was staring me in the face, though often the destination was nowhere in sight.

From the vantage point of retrospection, these times of hesitancy were acts of self-neglect and elongation of suffering.

I now know there was nothing to fear in *initiating action* if I placed my trust in it. It knew the pathways to heal grief better than I did. The commencements always frightened me because they loomed as lonely journeys into the unknown.

Once the threshold from revelation to *initiating action* was crossed, even timidly, the *action* seemed to take on a life of its own, in the same way as my heart pulses, my lungs breathe, my mind dreams, my memory reveals without being asked – my grief mysteriously healed.

Though grief was within me, it could never extinguish that inner light of provenance, imperceptibly revealing pathways as I stood on critical edges, prompting and guiding me to accept invitations to cross thresholds into the unknown, to the transformations and healings awaiting me, vital to the acceptance of the altered person I had become, to a sense of contentment.

It is the crossings, the leaps in faith, the *manifestations*, that forged the diminishment of my grief, over years.

3
The Claremont Serial Killings

The truth is, killing innocent people is always wrong and no argument or excuse, no matter how deeply believed, can ever make it right.

Feisal Abdul Rauf

The Claremont Serial Killings is the name given by the Australian media to the police case involving the disappearance of a young woman, and the killing of two other young women, in the period 1996–1997.

All three disappeared from the suburb of Claremont, Perth, Western Australia, in remarkably similar circumstances. Their disappearance and murders changed the landscape of Perth's night life, carved fear into the city's community, and is inscribed into the collective consciousness of all Western Australians.

This led the police to suspect a serial killer may be the offender.

The subsequent search for the killer was, up to the date of publication of this book, the largest, longest running and most costly murder investigation undertaken by any police force in Australia.

It commenced following the disappearance of the first woman, who was eighteen years old, on 27 January 1996. Her fate remains unknown, but she is presumed dead; her body has never been found.

The second woman, twenty-three years old, disappeared from the same part of Claremont on 9 June 1996. Her body, covered by branches from nearby shrubs, was discovered in Wellard, about forty kilometres south of Claremont, on 3 August 1996.

The third woman, twenty-seven years old, disappeared from Claremont on 15 March 1997. Her body, also partially concealed by branches from nearby shrubs and small trees, was found in Eglinton, a suburb about forty-five kilometres north of Claremont on 3 April 1997.

For all the tough times parents might confront in their lifetime, there can be nothing that comes even close to the loss of their child, especially in such circumstances.

The third woman was my oldest daughter, Ciara.

My remaining daughter, Denise, lost her best friend, her soulmate.

Twenty years after Ciara's murder, on 22 December 2016, a suspect was arrested in relation to the deaths of the second woman and Ciara. The next day he was charged with wilfully murdering both women. Following further investigation and consultation with the Director of Public Prosecutions, he was further charged with the wilful murder of the first woman on 22 February 2018. He was also charged in relation to earlier, separate attacks on two other women in Western Australia.

The first of these additional charges related to a house break-in, unlawful detention and deprivation of liberty of an eighteen-year-old woman, on 15 February 1988, in Huntingdale, a suburb forty kilometres south of Claremont.

The second charge was of abduction, unlawful detention and rape of a seventeen-year-old girl, on 12 February 1995, in Karrakatta, a suburb less than three kilometres from Claremont.

The suspect had earlier been charged with aggravated assault on a woman, on 7 May 1990, in Hollywood, a suburb adjacent to Claremont. He pleaded guilty to common assault on 1 June 1990 and was convicted and sentenced to two years probation.

He was charged with a total of eight offences, including the wilful murders of the first and second women and Ciara, on 22 February 2018. He remained in custody.

He unexpectedly pleaded guilty to the five non-murder charges on 21 October 2019.

Almost two years after the eight charges were laid, he was brought before a judge-only court. His trial commenced on 25 November 2019.

Following seven months of hearings, the trial finished on 25 June 2020.

On 24 September 2020, the judge handed down his 619-page verdict which found the suspect Bradley Edwards guilty of the murders of the second woman and Ciara, but not of the first woman due to insufficient evidence. The Judge stated the evidence of his propensity to kill may make Edwards a likely suspect, or even the probable killer, but did not exclude the real possibility that some other person killed her.

On 23 December 2020, Edwards was sentenced to life imprisonment with a minimum parole period of forty years, at that time the longest non-parole period sentence in the history of Western Australia.

Seven sentences, to be served concurrently, were handed down (numbered according to the charges laid):

1. Four years (Huntingdale offence – deprivation of liberty)

2. Two years (Huntingdale offence – breaking and entering dwelling with intent)

3. Three years (Karrakatta offence – deprivation of liberty)

4. Twelve years (Karrakatta offence – aggravated sexual penetration without consent)

5. Twelve years (Karrakatta offence – a second aggravated sexual penetration without consent)

6. Life, to serve a non-parole period of forty years (the murder of the second woman)

7. Life, to serve a non-parole period of forty years (the murder of Ciara).

A crucial factor in the conviction of Edwards was the sample of his DNA found under Ciara's fingernails, lodged there as she unsuccessfully fought to save her life, as he stabbed her to death.

He did not appeal the sentencing decision in the statutory time available to him.

The reasons for the more than thirty-year timespan between Edwards' first assault in 1988 and his sentencing in 2020 have been the subject of extensive reporting in Western Australian, national and international media, in several books published on the killings, in television coverage and documentaries, and social media worldwide.

In this book, I do not add to these reasons.

4
Ciara

The soul is healed by being with children.

Fyodor Dostoevsky

Ciara was born on 20 November 1969, in Zambia, and murdered on 15 March 1997.

Gone, not yet twenty-eight years of age.

Her first three years were spent in the company of Irish Sisters of Charity nuns and Zambians. Her early traits were understandably Irish, Christian. She learned to sing and dance shortly after she could walk. I can only connect her love of dance to a mysterious infusion of rhythm from her African nannies in her first five years.

Iona Primary School in Perth sowed the early seeds of her formal education, faith, love of ballet and sports, understanding of the value of friendship, sense of justice, and loyalty to friends. I cannot recall her ever criticising her friends. Many, scattered around the world, still regularly remain in contact with members of my family.

Before she was ten, her spirit of adventure emerged – secret bush hideaways, tearaway bicycle rides, exuberance in play, daring leaps from the highest diving board, swimming further from shore than most of her friends, a carefree and embracing laughter and free spirit.

She followed her own soul, wrote her own script.

During her five years in Iona College (high school), other attributes emerged. Her earlier love of ballet blossomed and her resolve to excel saw her having to choose between a professional ballet career or academic studies. Her self-discipline in ballet transferred to academic studies, intercollege athletics and a new interest in Japanese language and culture.

Her school life and eagerness for life, friends and faith were balanced, so well.

Following six years at the University of Western Australia, she graduated with a Bachelor of Arts (majoring in Japanese language) and a Bachelor of Laws.

During her university years, Ciara exemplified what all parents would like for their child.

She was a bright and healthy young woman with prospects of a successful legal career, plenty of friends, and a sunny outlook on the world. Her relationship with people endured. Friends cherished her friendship, as she did theirs.

At the end of her fourth year as a lawyer she took time out to travel overseas – Asia, Europe and America. Her regular telephone calls to assure me of her safety, share in her experiences and ease my concerns, at twenty-seven years of age, possibly seemed somewhat unnecessary to her at the time. Yet she did it.

Her visit to the Holy Land, especially Jerusalem, unveiled the values of her earlier education and confirmed her Christian faith.

The longer than planned stay in Ireland towards the end of her overseas travel was filled with celebration. She rediscovered her Celtic roots. The many beautiful memories she left with relatives now seem prophetic.

She returned home on 1 March 1997, to be bridesmaid at Denise's wedding, on 22 March 1997.

She was abducted and murdered on 15 March 1997.

Denise's wedding proceeded, as planned. Ciara was still missing.

Three weeks after her disappearance, in a business meeting, I received a call from a West Australian police officer. This was the call I had dreaded, knowing its content may hurtle me into a different world.

I stood at the precipice of hell unleashed.

Mr Glennon?

Yes.

The policeman's voice had a note of warning, but was slightly hesitant, as if to soften the blow.

We have found a body.

Yes.

We believe it may be your daughter.

I will never forget that call.

I informed Una.

I did not know what it meant, just experienced a feeling of the floor rapidly falling away, as if I had been standing on a trapdoor, suddenly opened. The ground I stood on before the call no longer existed.

The knot in my stomach had already conceived what I did not want.

Scarcely breathing. Eyes welled with tears. Mouth dry – cracked mud in what was once a lake.

Soon after, I discovered my daughter had been murdered in the most horrific of circumstances, causing an intense ghostly feeling that something inside me had been fractured, Ciara's absence haunting my heart.

I was advised not to view her body.

Knowing death with mind alone is not fully knowing it.

I never had the opportunity to see and touch the deadness of the daughter I loved.

Her murder ended a life full of hope.

A candle quenched.

Where has its light gone?

It is so profoundly WRONG for my child to be killed and die before me, and in such a horrific way.

As Nicholas Wolterstorff in his book, *Lament for a Son*, says: *It is the 'neverness' that is terrible; never again to see him.*

The solitude that accompanies that 'neverness' is a journey of woundedness, suffering, grief and survival.

There is no forgetting, always absence.

John O'Donohue in his book, *Walking in Wonder*, depicts absence: *absence is never clear-cut. Everyone that leaves your life leaves a subtle trail of connection with you; and when you think of them, and miss them and desire them, your heart journeys out again along that trail towards them in the elsewhere that they now find themselves.*

I remain vulnerable to her absence because I desire her presence so strongly.

What fills the emptiness of her absence is an aching.

Only my own death can truly stop the aching of her death.

5
Genesis of the Book

He who does not know how to look back at where he came from will never get to his destination

José Rizal

Prior to and after the publication of her book, *Ciara's Gift: Grief Edged with Gold,* in 2010, Una delivered approximately sixty talks to groups in metropolitan and rural centres in Western Australia and a number across Australia.

I attended many of the presentations, sitting alone at the back of the room, every time one of a handful of men, in audiences exceeding a hundred people.

At the end of some of the talks I was approached, privately, by a small number of attendees who had either lost a child or knew grief from a loss of another kind.

Never was there a question about grief from the loss of an elderly parent. Death is part of the normal process of living, but not when it is your child. We do not expect to bury our children.

All who had lost a child were experiencing the most painful, lasting and misunderstood grief.

The private comments and questions from women included:

My husband is overcome with grief, he has ceased being a father and husband. He has withdrawn into himself. It is terrible to watch. What can I do to help him? Where do I go for help?

Since we lost our son, my husband will not speak about it, to anyone, including me. I am concerned he is suffering from depression of some sort and may not recover. What can I do?

Our family business went into bankruptcy. My husband has lost his pride, feeling he has failed his family, especially his elderly parents, who are still alive. He has gone quiet. He refuses to talk about the loss of the business and is always angry with the bank. He is drinking more, much more. How long will this go on? Will he just keep going downhill? How long will it take for him to come out of it?

I lost my son to suicide. My daughter is dealing with it quite well. My other son, sixteen years old, lost his best friend and has withdrawn from life. He spends most of the time alone in his room. His school grades have dropped, and I am worried he will fall into depression. Where can I get help? How did your other daughter cope?

My child was murdered. His father and I separated some time ago. I am dealing with the grief, the police and the media on my own. The grief is hard enough. I do not trust the police because I feel they are not telling me the truth about the murder or how the investigation is going. They have not found the murderer. The suffering is just too much. Not knowing who killed my son is eating me away. What can I do to keep going, stay sane? How do I deal with the police? How do I deal with the media?

> *We lost our daughter to suicide. It was very public. The thoughtlessness of the media is never ending and their disregard for privacy is unbelievable. I cannot put up with any more of it. How do I deal with the media?*

> *Our daughter died from an overdose (of drugs). My husband now drinks, and watches sport all the time. I try to talk to him. He does not want to talk or listen. We go through the motions of living, looking after our other children. Will life ever get back to the way it was?*

> *My husband is drinking heavily since we lost our child. Will this continue and get worse? Did you drink more after you lost Ciara? Did Una and you deal with the loss of Ciara differently?*

The smaller number of men more hesitantly revealed or asked:

> *My daughter was killed in a car accident. I cannot stop thinking about her. Will I ever get a full night's sleep again? Will this suffering I am going through ever end? How long did it take you to get back to normal?*

> *Since the death of my son from a drug overdose, I find it hard just to get out of bed. I cannot face the hopeless place I am stuck in. I feel there is no point in trying to continue. Mostly I do not go to work. What can I do to move on and get back to work? How long did it take you to recover?*

> *I lost my son in an accident on our farm. I was with him at the time. I keep thinking I have let him and my family down. I am struggling with these guilty feelings. I am exhausted from no sleep. Will I ever get back to how I was before this happened? Did you feel the same when Ciara was murdered?*

Since I lost my child, if I continue like I am now, my family would be better off without me. I am just hopeless for them. I have lost the will to live. Is there somewhere I can get help? Did you look for medical or counselling help?

Why do my good friends not talk to me about my son's suicide? Many cross the road rather than say 'Hello'. My son and I were good friends; I miss him terribly. Will this loneliness ever go away? Will I ever stop thinking about him or crying when nobody is around?

Will you be able to forgive whoever murdered Ciara?

Since we lost our child, I am drained, cannot sleep. People telling me 'It's time to just move on with life' is not helpful. Were you the same? How did you manage?

I am a young father. I lost my daughter to cot death. It is just awful. Would you ever think about writing a book about how a father can deal with this nightmare – losing my child?

The organisers of Una's talks occasionally asked:

Would I speak to a group of men only?

Would I consider writing a book about how men can deal with grief, especially the grief from the loss of a child?

I agreed to speak and have done so on several occasions, to mixed groups.

The daunting task of writing a book – I put this aside for many years. I have now returned to it and to the questions asked by these people, all those years ago.

The genesis of the book is the combination of the questions asked at Una's talks and the dearth of writing by men about grief, particularly by men who have lost a child and write from a lived experience.

Grief never sleeps.

It has an ongoing propensity to overwhelm the mind, in the most surprising ways, at the most unexpected times; the indisputable head of obscurantism.

Before contemplating writing the book, I waited until I was certain I had found pathways to healings for my own grief, healings that had a rock-hard reliability, were enduring, were not a pretend way of living, but had created a permanent shift in my thinking.

I also waited until the person who murdered Ciara was found, arrested, charged, tried and sentenced, and is likely to be in prison for the remainder of his natural life.

Only then did I believe I might be able to write an authentic book, revealing the pathways I have discovered and walked. These pathways guided me to healings that have endured for two decades, and I am confident will not let me down during the times still to come.

6
The Readers I Had in Mind

There are some who bring a light so bright to our world that even when they are gone the light remains.

Unknown

Each parent's grief from losing a child is personal, inimitable.

The only genuine account any parent can give is their own.

Nobody can hazard a guess how another parent, in the same position, will deal with grief. It is unimaginable until it happens. All losses of a child are wounding and filled with suffering. Only the intensity and locale of the impacts varies.

Murder, whilst unfathomable, awful, is but one form of loss.

Yet the added complexities of the murder of a child are such that its abrupt nature, the intensity of the suffering of remaining family members, and the death at the hands of another make this grief different. There is well-researched evidence that families who have to deal with the violent death of a child experience severe psychological hurdles that have to be overcome.

Some chapters in this book are written in the first person. They describe my personal pathways through grief, towards the rebuilding of my life, to learn to walk with dignity and resilience.

I wrote the book with three broad categories of readers in mind:

1. A parent who has lost their child, for whatever reason.

2. A person in early or later grief caused by a significant loss in their life (other than the loss of their child).

3. Any parent seeking an understanding of what their spouse or partner is going through, wondering if they will ever recover from the grief to which he or she is a bewildered and frequently excluded witness, and how he or she might support the other whilst endeavouring to rebuild themselves.

   These parents are two people, doing their best to navigate through unfathomable grief that casts its dark and imprisoning shadow over whatever they do, think, feel and believe in. Their grief's interiority remains unrevealed, its emptiness continuing. Their thoughts and feelings are frequently kept secret, preferring isolation to consolation, and no spousal or public access to their individual thoughts, feelings or woundedness. Their only companionship is the dead self.

They may be parents seeking restored strength, courage and a helping hand, but possibly not admitting, even to themselves, that they need any of them.

They may be a parent collapsing into their own world of bewilderment and despair, seeking any hope and help they can to just survive.

Perhaps, if the helping hand extended to them is from another parent who:

> knows there are no deadlines when dealing with grief

has been pushed to the extremes of his resilience

knows there is a way back from the catastrophic loss

has stood in the darkness and returned with new understandings

has been at the tipping point of despair

temporarily lost courage

fought desperately to find the strength, determination and courage to get better

stepped back from the tipping point of desolation

found peace and contentment, amidst the chaos

walks harmoniously alongside the past, the present and the future (whatever the future may bring)

these parents may come to know *they are the caretakers of their own transfiguration, their own healing.*

If their grief is illuminated, its darker forces may no longer hold them prisoner.

My wish is that this book will be of assistance not only to parents but to anyone beset with grief who desperately wants nothing more than to be restored to a self who is at peace, or to find some contentment with where they find themselves.

I wrote the book in the hope that some fathers and mothers who have lost a child will find the words I have written resonate with their own thoughts, with their private battle, as they seek understanding on how to live with their grief, whilst wanting only to escape from it.

At the forefront of my mind were parents who find their grief incomprehensible, overwhelming, just too much, with no end in sight; who question whether returning to some form of normality is even possible.

The book may be helpful to parents who have dealt successfully and quickly with their grief and wonder if the brokenness they faced, and dealt with, was anything like that experienced by another parent thrown into the same chasm.

Other parents may have found an unexpected form of goodness in their grief, additional to the rebuilding of their life. Some others may cast the idea of finding any good in grief aside, convinced it is not remotely possible, thinking the prospect of finding any good in grief to be distasteful or even morally contradictory.

Throughout the writing of the book, the wives or partners of fathers were always in my mind. They are the ones whose 'strong man' has changed beyond recognition, been wounded, become a damaged replicate of the person they married or have known for so long.

Grief isolates him. His self-imposed seclusion is preferred to solace. Reasons for his woundedness remain unspoken. Stoic tearlessness prevails. His feelings are lidded. Suffering remains masked; even though it is hard to hide, he does his best to mask it.

The child they both loved will never again be with them and nothing will fill the void of this absence.

These women can be the ones left to 'pick up the pieces' in a family that has been badly broken. I hope my words may shine some luminous light into the darkness of the altered world in which these strong women find themselves.

The book may offer a cord of understanding to surviving siblings who are in their own state of sadness, wondering if the strong, happy father and/or mother they knew and admired will ever re-emerge. Will they ever become strong enough to be again 'Mum' and 'Dad'?

Men are not good at talking about this stuff, but sometimes words are not needed.

People, even friends, are incapable of finding words for this kind of grief. About three weeks after Ciara's funeral I met a close friend at my yacht club. We both paused. He hesitantly held out his hand. I took it, waiting for him to speak. Words just fell away. Before hastily withdrawing his hand, as his eyes welled with tears, he gently, momentarily squeezed my hand. Without a single spoken word, a silent act of understanding and kindness by one man to another. When I'm low I always think of that wordless gesture and the uplifting feeling it gave me. I would like him to read my book, but unfortunately he unexpectedly passed away shortly after our brief encounter.

This is a personal and frank book, recognising always that each person's grief is unique, even though our grief may hold strong similarities.

I have written from a broad Christian perspective, for parents who have lost too much and are unsure how to navigate life where a void has opened, and who are in grief. If you are a father or mother who has lost a child, I hope this book may go some way to fill that void.

I stared into the same empty space, too many times.

If you come from a different faith, or perhaps no faith at all, the chapter on Spiritual Impacts and Transcendence was not included to cause offence or push a particular view. Far from it.

The intent, always, was to extend hope and harmony, not despair or discontent.

As I wrote, I felt on more than one occasion that the words, as they unfolded on the page, were unwinding the bandages that still cover my own grief.

I have learned and been granted insights to glimpses of wisdom and flashes of deeper truth about my grief. I have learned to live with it, in the best peace possible, with a newly found and undeniable sense of contentment.

It is my fervent belief that all grieving parents can discover similar pathways.

PART II

7
A Lens on My Early Grief

You may not be interested in grief, but grief is interested in you.

with apologies to Leon Trotsky

When Ciara was murdered, I lost not only my child but also the part of me she represented. I lost the future we may have made together. This is not the aspiration of academic, social or professional success that I may have harboured for her. It is about being together in the future as we were in the past, only more so as we became 'friends', beyond being 'father and daughter'.

Her murder is so final, it has subjected me to feelings of loss unlike any other experience in my life, before or since. The murder of our child is a violation of everything we believe to be just, decent and honest, or expect in life.

How easily we can be besieged, deadened. How powerless we are. There are no practice runs to get to know this kind of grief.

The physical, psychological, emotional and spiritual impacts defy whole understanding.

The grief from the loss of the child I parented pounded body, mind, heart and spirit. It will rattle the strongest parent.

The grief is inundated with emptiness and helplessness, and brings physical distress, spiritual filleting, and feelings of spiritual abandonment.

Time crawls. Nights are long, dark times.

The grief during the three weeks Ciara was missing was buried beneath distress, disbelief, denial, despair, powerlessness, nausea, anger and sheer exhaustion from lack of sleep.

I walked inside an incomprehensible, dreadful dream. Any minute I would force myself to wake up and none of it would have happened. Ciara would be found alive.

Not so.

When her body was found, I had to accept she was gone.

My vision of us being together in the future was annihilated.

She was dead.

Parts of me died too.

The agony became what I thought then was insufferable.

I had no idea what was to be let loose.

Having obtained the appropriate permissions, I read the autopsy report revealing the circumstances of her murder as soon as it was compiled.

The photographs were graphic, indelible in my memory.

I knew then how Ciara died. These images are burned into my consciousness. Hiding my eyes with my hands, I still recoil. How could any man murder a young woman, like Ciara was murdered? Her last minutes or hours would have been terrifying for her.

It was a long time before I could shut my eyes and not see her as her murderer had left her, covered with scrub and branches to conceal her.

What man-monster could do this?

Those early days and endless nights are a blur. I thought each dawn would never come. When it came, it broke only on tear-filled absences and more heartbrokenness. The early days of grief are tough. They are just day-to-day survival.

Before Ciara's death I had not experienced family grief, nor even been close to it. Its intensity came as a complete shock to me. At her funeral, I did not place the traditional handful of soil on her coffin. It was too difficult.

The reality of what had happened to her was no longer avoidable.

From that morning onwards, psychological denial as a protective shield was stripped back, exposing raw woundedness of mind and body. The loss of Ciara was more than I could bear.

The early grief was amplified by confusion and feelings of anger, the likes of which I had not known I owned. I felt anger towards the murderer, the police and the local council, who (in my view) had not done enough to address safety and security measures in Claremont following the earlier disappearance of two other women in similar circumstances.

The psychological disharmony of what had happened ate into the very core of who I was. There are no rules, no timetables, no explanations, no linear pathway and no known end for this kind of grief.

Suffering that is not understood is particularly hard to bear.

I directed some of my greatest anger and interrogations towards the God I believed in, firing my questions at Him:

> Why do you let bad things happen to good people?
>
> What have I done, or not done, to deserve this?
>
> Why am I being treated so cruelly?
>
> Is this punishment for something I did or didn't do?
>
> Where were you when Ciara was murdered?
>
> Why did you not reach down and stop it? She was a good person.
>
> How could you let this happen if you are a loving and caring God?
>
> Do you even care?
>
> We prayed for Ciara's safe return; why were our prayers not answered?
>
> How can I continue to believe in you – the just God I was brought up to trust in?
>
> What kind of world did you create, in which these horrific things happen?

This spiritual turmoil called the basic tenets of my faith into question. It was distinct from the physical exhaustion, the psychological confusion and emotional heartbrokenness that came from experiencing for the first time a profound sense of abandonment by God.

Do atheists or agnostics wrestle with these spiritual questions? I don't know, but think not.

The spiritual impacts of grief bring an added layer to believers, no matter the name they give their God.

My Catholic faith offered no insurance against being powerless and helpless in the face of this tragedy. Nor did my faith initially offer protection against the early feelings of spiritual abandonment, distrust and apparent betrayal. If anything, being a Catholic, in unforeseen ways, complicated my attempts to come to grips with the evil of what had happened.

During those early times, it was difficult to continue to believe in any form of Superior Being.

I call that Being, God.

If you are a believer, please call it whatever you wish, or no name at all.

I cannot remember feeling any spiritual presence at that time.

It was difficult to find prayerful words.

I was just fixated on survival.

8
Early Searching for Sources of Help

Maybe you are searching among the branches,
for what only appears in the roots.

Rumi

Three or four months after Ciara's funeral I started searching for books and other information on grief that might help make sense of the uncharted hell I found myself in. The books or literature I found then available fell in four broad categories.

Books describing stages of grief

The most well known of these is the book by the Swiss psychiatrist Elizabeth Kübler-Ross, *On Death and Dying*, in which she describes five distinct stages (denial, anger, bargaining, depression and acceptance) that she proffered people in grief go through. Other authors have since dissected this model, whilst others have expanded it to seven or more stages.

My response to Ciara's murder, most times, unfolded differently to what the Kübler-Ross model postulated. There were no discrete stages that I could discern. There was no linear order to the progress of my grief.

Rabbi Harold Kushner's book, *Why Bad Things Happen to Good People*

This book is dedicated to Kushner's son, who died in 1977 from an incurable genetic disease.

Rabbi Kushner sought to answer what I then thought were the unanswerable questions:

> *Why God did you let this happen to me, a good and faithful servant?*
>
> *If the God I believe in is so omnipotent, omnibenevolent, good and loving, why does he allow so much suffering and evil in the world, in my world?*

Like Kushner, I believe in God. His questions were the same as mine. In parts, the book was reassuring in that it attempted to provide an explanation for the core spiritual question on grief: *Why am I, a believer, suffering so savagely and so intensely?*

For Christians, or believers in any form of God, their faith can be a double-edged sword: comforting and heartening, but also leading to anguish and feelings of abandonment and disenchantment, especially at a time you need help the most. I read this book three times, hopeful I could find a purpose to my grief, so that I could bear it more easily. In a general way, this book was helpful.

But the words of the Nobel laureate physicist Steven Weinberg are relevant: *If there is a God that has special plans for humans, then He has taken very great pains to hide His concern for us.*

I then related to Weinberg's words.

Books and articles written by professionals

These publications are authored by grief counsellors, grief therapists, psychotherapists, psychologists and other people offering grief support. Then and now, a search for the most frequently recommended books on grief reveals the vast majority are authored by women. Several such books are listed in the Bibliography.

Many groups have been established to aid grieving individuals or families. I did not conduct extensive reading of the material published by such groups as much of the material and the services offered (at least to me) concentrated on analysis of grief, in workshops, small groups or one-on-one sessions, and offering 'strategies' or 'toolkits,' directed at a general audience of people suffering from a wide spectrum of grief.

My decision, early in grief, not to use the services of such groups, or services linked to individual churches, specialist grief counsellors or grief therapists, curtailed my exploration of potential help from these sources.

Papers and research articles by academics on more abstract aspects of grief

Some of these topics were:

- adaptation of the body or mind during grief
- cardiovascular events during acute grief
- changes in biomarkers during grief
- differences between mothers and fathers of deceased children

gender differences in adjustment to grief

historical developments in bereavement research

the neurobiology of grief

and more theoretical dissections of the suffering processes associated with grief, from whatever cause.

My search for helpful books and literature, at that time, revealed there was a dearth of material on grief written by men. A number of publications covered the grief experienced by couples. When fathers were mentioned in these publications, most wrote about how the husband/partner might help his wife/partner through the heartbreak of it all. This is not a critique; it's just the way I found it, as did others.

Mark Seidman in his book, *Grieving Dad: Surviving and Healing the Loss of Your Child*, says:

> *When I went searching, I found lots of books on grieving. Many were written by women, some of whom were moms who had lost their children. Others were written by men, but most were psychologists and other 'experts' who had not personally experienced this unimaginable loss. I did find one or two books by men who had lost children that chronicled their experiences, but I never found a book written by a dad for dads that outlined steps I could take to find my way out of the black hole of gloom that surrounded me.*

Kelly Farley with David DiCola in their book, *Grieving Dads: To the Brink and Back*, write:

Almost all of the resources I could find on the subject of grieving for a child was directed either toward women or 'parents.' I put 'parents' in quotation marks, because in my experience, most of what I read for grieving parents was written for mothers. If I did come across something aimed at grieving dads, it was usually advice about how to comfort their wives.

The high proportion of female authors and researchers has since shifted, but marginally. At the time of publication of this book, there is still an exceedingly small number of publications by men. Some of these are listed in the Bibliography.

What has certainly changed, particularly in the last ten years, is the proliferation of publications dealing specifically with grief.

However, the greatest discovery from searching the grief literature was unforeseen. The reading of such material did not hasten the healing of the impacts of the grief I experienced. Instead, the constant searching for answers removed me from what the grief itself might teach me.

My mind was a dark room into which I shovelled everything I could read on grief, hoping that light might get in. Working, working at it, I was in control of the process. No loosening, no losing. How wrong I was.

A true meaning of grief cannot be discovered in academic theory or cold analyses, or in the writings of others.

The best answers were inside myself, yet to rise within me, even though, at that time, it was hard to believe that hidden in the heart of my grief, there may be light; there may be healings.

This discernment demanded a 180-degree turn, underpinned by a mental toughness, a bloody-minded determination and lots of courage, to not get hung up on the models or process of grief articulated in the writings of others, otherwise they become the main focus. I was not going to be preoccupied with functional reasoning, which sees everything in terms of a process, stages, rationality and mathematical/statistical endorsement for validity.

I had to be open to the possibility of divine pathways, at least some of the time.

My soul, on occasions, guided the choreographer of pathways towards healings, prompting me at least now and again to visit that inner sanctuary.

Nelson Mandela's words, quoted by poet John O'Donohue are relevant: *You know what we are afraid of is not so much our limitations, but the infinite within us.*

I ceased reading for several years.

It was through a tough, dedicated personal exploration of my grief's impacts that light shone on narrow pathways, inviting me, guiding me forward, to a transfiguration of grief.

9

Understanding the Grief from the Loss of a Child Requires Work, but Can Be Done

Only people who are capable of loving strongly can also suffer great sorrow, but this same necessity of loving serves to counteract their grief and heals them.

Leo Tolstoy

To dispel any uncertainty, this is not a 'how to' book to survive grief. It is not a 'practical guide' to dealing with thc wilderness of grief. It does not provide 'toolkits' or 'strategies' for parents or others in grief.

It just tells the story of how I dealt with my own grief and how I found peace and contentment.

Grieving is hard, exhausting work, but can be done by all with dignity.

Grief's impacts on different people will long be debated. But the impacts of grief on a parent who has lost their child, being at the top of the list, is not a matter of debate; this is well documented.

This type of grief was physically, psychologically, emotionally and spiritually tough and tortuous, no matter how strong I thought I was. Before that, I went through life under the illusion I was *in control* and if I pushed hard enough, life would yield to my will.

Ciara's murder, especially that it happened in such unforeseen and violent circumstances, mocked the idea of control.

The woundedness and suffering uncovered my vulnerability; we really have no control over what can happen in life.

This raw and unpleasant truth demanded frank acknowledgement before I could conceive of any healing.

It was only when I moved forward from the early times of just surviving that I could ask the question:

Now that I have to accept Ciara is never coming back, what do I do with the woundedness, suffering and grief, none of which are receding and, if I am honest with myself, over which I had no control to stop in the first instance?

The moving from *just surviving* to *healing*, to *living with grief*, can take a long time. For some parents, years, but for all parents it is achievable.

The quote by thirteenth-century poet Rumi, *Suffering is a gift. In it is hidden mercy*, makes no sense to a parent trying to just survive the early times of grief. I shook my head in disbelief when I first read this quote. I thought it was cruel. There was no *gift* or *hidden mercy* in what I was going through.

The thought of grief being somehow good is an oxymoron.

Despite my view, the untangling of the paradox of the suffering caused by grief requires a reconciliation of two dichotomous viewpoints:

> *Grief has some good*, at least according to the poet Rumi and others.

Grief has no good, is too hard and should be avoided. This was my reaction and I guess is the natural reaction of all parents who have lost a child.

Whatever good grief may provide, for me it could never surpass its detrimental hurt. I still find it nigh impossible to accept that any good can come from grief.

Initially, the despair brought into sharp focus the multifaceted impacts of grief: awareness of the transience of life; debilitating apprehension and sorrow; the emptiness of being ring-fenced by anguish; wanting to avoid thinking about it; running from the past; hiding from the future; having no control over what will happen in life.

I realised I had little option but to give attention to these impacts, see them for what they were, and understand the nature of them before any process of healing or moving forward could take place.

Loss, woundedness, suffering, grief and healing do not suddenly become *best friends.*

I had no idea from where, or how, I could find the strength, determination, courage or wisdom to move forward, towards any healing.

Yet one night, no sleep, wide awake, an insight was revealed:

I had no choice but to resign myself to having to face my grief, somehow learning to live with it, and stop wishing for it to miraculously disappear. It was not going anywhere.

For any understanding of how an integration of grief might be attainable, I had to be open to this possibility. This was not an easy line for me to cross.

The work on this was very slow; taking one step forward, being pushed three steps back. I read what I could readily find on how to deal with grief, hoping that learning from others might help.

Several authors preceded me.

Holocaust survivor Victor Frankl in *Man's Search for Meaning*:

> *For what matters above all is the attitude we take towards suffering, the attitude in which we take our suffering upon ourselves.* ***Suffering ceases to be suffering in some way in the moment that it finds a meaning.***

This made some sense to me, conceptually.

Donald Kalsched in *Trauma and the Soul*:

> *In those places where we are broken, we may be graced again with the experience of wholeness. But if this is to happen, we will have to* **permit ourselves to surrender to the broken places** *again, now surrounded by a thornbush of defences, ready to shoot poison darts at us if we try. Sometimes our courage fails us,* **and we are not up to the surrender**. *Then life's tragedies are left to break us open once again, giving us a glimpse of the lost wholeness, however ambivalent we may be about it.*

What 'broken places' must I surrender to? There were so many places in me already broken. To what more did I need to surrender? How little I knew!

Miriam Greenspan, in *Healing Through the Dark Emotions*, says: *Instead of 'turning away' from pain we can learn* **to gently, slowly, mindfully,**

***and incrementally 'turn towards'** or lean into the discomfort we're experiencing.*

Why the need to 'lean into' my suffering? I felt everything it hit me with, without getting any closer to it. I wanted it to go away. I wanted to run away from it.

David Roland in *The Power of Suffering*:

> *In remaking ourselves, we are adjusting to a world that is not how it was, or how we would like it to be. Following a life trauma, we need* ***to find new meaning****, new purpose,* ***new understanding, new relationships, new accommodations*** *to the physical or mental limitations, or to the loss that has ensnared us.* ***It is the grappling with*** *how to become whole again when this injury, devastation or grief has torn us apart that* ***we need to negotiate****. The struggle that suffering presents is to be embraced in all its thorniness;* ***acceptance is the first step in moving on****. The prize on offer for doing so is the transformation into someone new – maybe someone even better than before.*

New meaning, new purpose, new understanding, new relationships, new accommodations – so much to find! But from where and how?

Megan Devine's book, *It's OK that You're not OK*:

> *Some things cannot be fixed. They can only be carried.*
>
> *This book is about how you live inside your loss.* ***How you carry what cannot be fixed.*** *How you survive.*
>
> *Loss gets integrated, not overcome.*

This also made more sense to me, especially the idea that *grief cannot be fixed*. That is precisely how I felt.

C.S. Lewis in *The Problem of Pain*: *Pain provides* **an opportunity for heroism**; *the opportunity is seized with surprising frequency.*

This notion was a step too far, for me; still is.

Randy Pausch in *The Last Lecture*: *We cannot change the cards we are dealt, just how we play the hand.*

Nancee Sobonya, creator of the documentary *The Gifts of Grief*, says:

> *Many times grief unmasks us, and we are stripped down to our real, vulnerable self...As the loss burns and the waves of grief crash through them,* **some people discover something inside themselves** *that they never knew existed – a depth of compassion, of* **understanding**, *of* **strength** *and* **courage**, *a connection with humanity.*

What I most needed was restored strength, more courage and more determination to keep getting up each morning, to keep stepping forward, looking for steppingstones anywhere, everywhere.

Deborah Spungen, mother of a murdered child, in her book, *Homicide: The Hidden Victims*, states:

> *In the aftermath of a homicide, the co-victims are often involved in various activities imposed on them by the medical examiner, the criminal justice system, and possibly the media. This is true whether or not an arrest is made.* **Such involvement is not by choice, and these endeavours are time consuming, physically and emotionally exhausting, and sometimes quite public.**

Co-victims are left with little energy to traverse the rest of the grief process, which is distinct from the experience by those whose loved one did not die violently. As a result, co-victims may be incapable of moving on to other phases until there is some finality to the legal aspects of the case, such as the completion of the trial.

I related very much to these comments but at the time I had no concept of how applicable and hurtful they would become for me, many years later.

The potent parallels in what each of these authors expressed were undeniable.

I found a sense of comfort in finding words expressed so perfectly by another, they could be found in my own soul.

I became more knowledgeable about the concepts of *facing grief head on, accepting grief, carrying grief, living with grief, integrating grief*, but at that time, after much reading, I still had no chart to navigate a way forward and didn't know what to do with my own grief. The most elusive and most difficult to understand was the concept of integrating grief. In the end, I decided it was the permanent incorporation of grief into who I had become and I would never be able to excise it from the core of my being.

This was not a disappointment. It was a reality. I had to be open to sources beyond the literature.

I again stopped reading – this break lasted several years.

When I ceased searching for answers in the writings of others, an insight transpired. I concluded that reading about others' suffering and grief is one thing, but any practical knowledge of how to *lean into it, fit it in, carry it, integrate it* into my changed life and, worst of all, *continue to live with it*, was absent, at best vague, even mysterious.

This required a deeper examination of my understanding of the grief I was experiencing – its ever present *physical, psychological, emotional* and *spiritual* impacts on me – but an examination with an open heart and a watchful reverence of what might be revealed to me.

My attempt to identify and categorise the impacts, the prerequisite for examination, is outlined in the next chapter. The attempt is not perfect, but it helped me.

If I teased these impacts out, being open to insights that might be transformed into manifestations of healing, perhaps I would find pathways forward that were my own, not caricatures of others.

10
Impacts of Grief – A Personal Perspective

Though nothing can bring back the hour of splendour in the grass,
of glory in the flower, we will grieve not,
rather find strength in what remains behind.

William Wordsworth

Grief brings wounds, hurts, injuries, damage and suffering – these are the 'impacts' of grief.

The mosaic of impacts each person experiences differs only in intensity and locale, each impact callously prolonging healing, as if some vital essence or core is being continuously siphoned out.

There is no place the loss of Ciara has not touched – body, mind, heart and spirit have all been impacted. The impacts can be separated and allocated to four, interwoven, dimensions:

physical – *body*
psychological – *mind*
emotional – *heart*
spiritual – *spirit* or *soul*

Agnostics or nonbelievers may not accept, or agree with, the inclusion of the spiritual impacts and select to confine their reading to the other three; I respect everyone's image of their godhead or no godhead.

The four dimensions are inextricably interlacing, overlapping and interdependent. The boundaries between the impacts are porous, not impervious. The impacts are not imprisoned inside a single dimension; they mix like clouds. Several impacts, not unexpectedly, surface in more than one dimension.

Fatigue, anxiety or panic may be experienced physically and psychologically; fear may be experienced emotionally and psychologically; cognitive dysfunction may be experienced psychologically and spiritually. This is not surprising as we are speaking about the organic makeup of a person.

The predominant impacts I experienced are listed below. These are the only ones of which I can speak authentically.

Physical impacts: withdrawal from life; no determination to push on; sleep disturbance; loss of appetite; lethargy; muscle tension; fatigue; uncontrollable crying; palpitations; nausea; stress; weighed down as if I was wearing a heavy, soaking wet blanket that smothered me.

Psychological impacts: disbelief; denial; nightmares of Ciara's last minutes; inability to concentrate; sense of control in life gone; addled brain; barrages of cyclic anxieties; forgetfulness; memory gaps; assault of unanswerable questions; cognitive dysfunction; avoiding mourning; flashbacks; sense of injustice.

Emotional impacts: sadness; guilt; shock; anger; resentment; apathy towards people and life; loneliness; fear; absence of joy; loss of trust; numbness; helplessness; yearning; despair; purposelessness; absence of peace; no feelings of contentment.

Spiritual impacts: spiritual doubts and questions about God's goodness; confronting and rethinking of basic beliefs in God; spiritual abandonment; emptiness with regards to religion and its rituals; questioning the meaning of suffering; fracturing of the intactness of my spiritual life; spiritual numbness; no mortal answers in my faith; no protection from the suffering provided by my faith.

The allocation of the impacts to a particular dimension is arbitrary and personal. I respect that each person's grief is as unique as their fingerprints.

Psychologists and psychiatrists with an interest in grief, grief counsellors and grief therapists may select different or additional impacts and may allocate them differently. I did not experience all impacts simultaneously, but each was encountered, at varying intensities and differing times, over the hours, days, nights, weeks, months and years.

Rarely did I find that the dimensions of grief or its impacts listed by academic researchers or professional counsellors were derived from *a lived experience* of their own grief. Again, this is not a critique; it's what I found.

The only ones who entirely understand grief are those who have lived through it.

Understanding is required of how these impacts persistently permeate our very core. We seek insights and revelations to illuminate pathways towards an amelioration of the potency of these impacts to weaken and damage us. We need to be open to these insights or revelations, to recognise them, and initiate actions needed to transform them into the manifestations that bring healing. It is a journey through valleys and across mountains, where, in the early days, we live life as best we can, without knowing how our grief will end, or how we will survive.

Yet there is no doubt in my mind it is a journey that can be walked by all parents and others in grief who are open to putting in the work, to push on against big odds, and become strong again. This can take years, but the rewards are invaluable, incalculable.

Have I reached a sheltered harbour of calm waters and found some peace, some contentment following Ciara's murder?

Yes.

Have I emerged a *changed* person? Of this, I have no doubt.

Have I *changed for the better* as a human being? I believe so.

But, in the blink of an eye, I would trade these changes to have Ciara back.

Given that this is not possible, I am grateful for: finding ways to discern and understand the impacts of grief and the discovery of pathways to heal them; the rebuilding of my life; the authentic acceptance of my grief; the degree of contentment I now have.

The next six chapters describe the pathways I found, and followed, to discern the impotence buried within the impacts of each dimension of grief, rather than being constantly overwhelmed by them. Discovery of impotence leads to surprising healings.

I needed the totality of the healing to live with grief, be at peace with the altered person I have become, and know contentment in my altered landscape.

It is the inner human landscape of my search for knowledge, integration of same, healing, rich friendship and companionship where I dare to be free, my heart can be nourished, my soul can shelter, home to the hearth of my own spirit; the home where grief now resides only in the lowlands of my life.

11
Physical Impacts and Inner Strength

We need the iron qualities that goes with manhood. We need the positive virtues of resolution, of courage, of indomitable will, of power to do without shrinking the rough work that must always be done.

Theodore Roosevelt

In the early months after Ciara's murder, every morning, and several times every day, I asked:

Why push on? If this is what life is about, why bother?

As I tried to sleep, most times turmoil intruded. Minutes turned into hours.

I frequently recalled the words of the Russian playwright Anton Chekhov: *Any idiot can face a crisis, it is the day-to-day living that wears you out.*

On most early days, my skin quivered with the destabilising, relentless assault of grief on my body.

A veil of hurt and loss came between my family and me, and between me and some of my friends. I witnessed what Una was going through. Her cross was much heavier than mine. I could not lean on her. My remaining daughter was trying to deal with the loss of her sister and best friend.

Unlike popular thought, the loss of a child, no matter the reason for the loss and the resultant grief, do not necessarily, initially, draw the remaining members of a family closer.

Strangers, friends, business colleagues and neighbours offered their support. In their midst, the exhaustion, lethargy and heartache persisted. It seemed an eternity since I felt strong and had any determination or courage to keep going.

I returned to work within three weeks of Ciara's funeral.

Despite the weight of grief pushing me down, I kept thinking, saying, repeating to myself, *I am not going to take this grief lying down*. Somehow I had to find the physical strength, the mental toughness, the determination and the courage to get on top of it.

From somewhere, I slowly experienced small increases in *mental toughness* to push on. I do not know if this is the same as willpower. This increased *mental toughness and determination*, no matter how tiny, were welcomed.

They gave me a little more strength to get out of bed, walk through the day. They also encouraged me to recognise new *shimmers of courage*, which refused to be extinguished by what had happened.

When the increased *toughness and determination* stirred inside me, they restored, not every time, a little more *physical strength*, a little *greater courage*. It felt as if the grief was being transformed to *toughness and determination* and *greater courage*. It was not a straightforward process, and it did not happen in neat or in predictable steps.

The effort to find this *mental toughness, restored strength, increased determination* and *greater courage* is quite different to the conscious effort we put into gym work, or another training activity, to develop physical strength and increase our resolve to win.

We measure the results of gym work and other training in well-tested metrics – muscle enhancement and level of fitness. We run faster, swim longer, jump higher, lift more, break records. The physical strength from this kind of premeditated effort is steadily built up. We know if we train, we will improve performance. Entry to this type of improvement of physical self is *voluntary*.

A parent who has lost their child is physically drained at the time grief strikes their body. No amount of gym work or other physical exercise or training can help them 'get off their knees', 'face the day', 'get back into life', 'stop the sorrow', 'overcome the physical impacts assaulting them'. Their entry to this world, of grief, has been *involuntary*.

The *mental toughness, determination,* and *courage* I speak of can only come from within us. They are not easily measurable, but their presence and power to strengthen us are indisputable. No doctor, counsellor, psychologist or psychiatrist can write a prescription to assist this kind of physical strengthening. But we require it when intense grief smashes our lives.

David Roland, in his book *The Power of Suffering*, states this requirement more forcefully: ***bloody-minded*** *determination is required* .

From where to find these attributes remained vague, yet I resolved to lead my family out of what had happened to us.

Taking care of my family was, by far, my number one priority, no matter the personal cost.

The insight into how to do this was revealed serendipitously and unexpectedly when I was at one of my lowest points, on my knees, imploring for the strength, from anywhere, to push on, find a pathway forward, get on top of the grief, head my family, lead my family, take care of my family.

Out of grief rose a long-buried, trustworthy clarity of thought. It revealed a pathway.

So much depends on our frame of vision – the window through which we look at our circumstances in life.

12
Fear a'tidgh

But there is no need to be ashamed of tears, for tears bore witness that a man had the greatest of courage, the courage to suffer.

Viktor E Frankl, *Man's Search for Meaning*

Fear a'tidgh (pronounced 'far a tigh') is a Gaelic expression with deep meaning and long history in Irish family culture.

The closest translation to English is 'man of the house'.

In today's world of gender equality, the concept and term may be regarded by some as old-fashioned, possibly inappropriate or unacceptable. Others may consider the notion to be redundant, having little legitimacy in our current world of gender equality and fluidity. I have no issues with such views.

But that is not the culture or home environment in which I lived for the first twenty-six years of my life.

I was born into a traditional Irish family, the oldest of seven children: my mother, the full-time homemaker; my father, the breadwinner and the respected *man of the house*, the *head of the family*.

His mother, my grandmother, had eleven children. A woman of powerful spirit, equal in every way to her husband, my grandfather. He was the acknowledged *head* of the wider Glennon clan.

I admired my grandfather and father greatly. I was raised in the shadow of both. They were strong, humble men who valued putting themselves second to others. They were always quiet in a clan gathering but we listened when they spoke.

They were not daunting figures of righteousness or stern men. Their courage was never pretentious, but it was never lacking or found wanting. They were determined, dependable, soft-spoken men, an abandonment of their family beyond their thinking. They were men their wives and families could rely on, until death parted them.

Both headed their families by cultivating an unspoken, quiet, nurturing atmosphere of family cohesion, friendship, manners, fairness, truthfulness, decency, an honourable work ethic, competitive sportsmanship, a respect for others and a spiritual base in their respective homes – unwritten, never doubted, accepted and respected values.

They instilled in me a sense of obligation that when my time came, I too should assume the responsibility of being *head* of my own family. This obligation and its accompanying values were not founded on a *set of rules* my father or grandfather had conceived. The values they passed to me were the same as had been handed to them. They were not about power, control, status, special authority, commanding or demanding respect, being in charge, condescension, other members of the family being second class, or being granted some sort of superiority – all caricatures of the real meaning.

They were about knowing the importance of embracing responsibility and there was never a thought that my sister or female cousins were any less able or lesser human beings.

The *fear a'tidgh* values, as if guided by an unseen celestial hand, were deftly conveyed from father to son – a true companion to all men who have the good fortune to have been moulded from the clay of a good father. These are values, enforced with sinews of steel, that sons don't know exist until they have to reach deep for them, forever finding them trustworthy and enduring.

No demands were made of me, no instructions were given to me, no promises were extracted from me. The expectation was just instilled in me; never lectured, just unconsciously understood. I imitated what I observed and experienced. In it, too, resides an ineffable friendship where you feel belonging and affinity.

What has all this got to do with losing Ciara and the physical impacts of grief?

For three months or so after Ciara's funeral, I struggled to get out of bed, face the day, go to work, withstand the onslaught of the continuous waves of grief.

The yearnings to remain strong, have the determination and courage, were genuine and constant, but the *how* to convert these yearnings into a reality was absent. The pathway to initiate the action remained concealed.

On many weekends, I withdrew to the sanctuary of our yacht, *Calypso V*. I would just say to Una: *I'm going to the boat*. She guessed or knew why.

There, alone in the aft cabin, I would cry uncontrollably for hours, trying to make sense of the change in our lives and the loss of Ciara. This crying is seismic, an inkling of the depth from which it erupts. I wept internally, convulsing, tears or no tears, at times just dry heaving.

Deep crying was my body's initial instinctive antidote to the loss of Ciara. It was nature's medication when my world had fallen apart.

The visits to the yacht continued over several months, each time alone, no spoken words from another. There were no consoling words when I was doubled over by the crushing weight of grief.

The unthinkable of losing Ciara had become the thinkable. The minutes, hours and evenings passed, they seemed to stretch into an eternal frozen present. Many times I felt I may not come out of it at all, and that I was on a downward slippery slope to God's know where. I had collapsed into sorrow.

On one evening, through tears, I thought for the first time since Ciara was murdered of my father and grandfather.

I asked: *How would these men deal with what has happened to my family, to me?*

I had never seen either man cry.

I shuddered as if I had received a mild electric shock. My body trembled and I felt a power yanking me out of the depths, out of the physical impacts of grief. The force lifting me seemed unlike that which I could attribute to a human hand. It was intervening to help me get off my knees. Stand up. Be strong. Be the *head of my family.*

In a confused state of incredulity and appreciation, whilst I was undergoing a pounding from the physical impacts of intense grief, I was now being assisted to clamber out.

I did not move for I do not know how long. I just lay there, exhausted.

Silence pervaded the whole aft cabin.

Something deep inside me, the bedrock, had shifted.

Feelings and thoughts of increased *mental toughness* and *physical strength*, together with an *implacable determination* and a *greater courage* surfaced from somewhere within, compelling me to stand up, face the physical impacts for what they were, find ways to lessen their injurious wounding, remain strong, carry on, walk tall.

It is what my father and grandfather would have expected of me if they were present.

The pathway forward was revealed.

Brittle manhood bones were fleshed with insight, torn flesh was stitched, and healing happened.

The manifestation of the insight was the instant formation of the inner *mental toughness* and *implacable determination* I was seeking.

I knew what I had to *do*.

I do not know where these wellsprings lie in us.

I surrendered to the unambiguity of the shift, to its feeling of inner strength and sense of purpose.

I have no rational explanation for the *restored physical strength*, just as I don't have for the resolute *mental toughness*, *determination* and *courage* that manifested themselves.

It is hard to hear the softest of voices in a space filled with the clamouring of uncontrollable crying.

Only in stillness can the inner voices be heard.

My mind moved from despondency to certainty. I now knew I could physically hold up my end, initiate the necessary action, do the work and remain strong, to lead my family in my altered life.

I immediately resolved I would do whatever it took to find the person who murdered Ciara, or I would die trying. The next day I visited Ciara's grave, alone, and made that private promise to her.

By mysteriously drawing from the inherited *fear a'tidgh* values, buried within me, came the increased strength to face and deal with the physical impacts of my grief.

All fathers long to be connected to wise, worthy, faithful, strong values; to look after our own and ourselves. Fathers want to know these values and their purpose, despite the mysteriousness of their genesis. They are buried somewhere inside us, waiting for the time we need to call on them.

When Ciara was murdered, my world exploded beneath me, yet this same detonation revealed the validity of the *fear a'tidgh* values, their inner strength.

Why did it take desolation to reveal the healing nature of these childhood learnings? Why was the elemental purpose of these values manifested so starkly only when I could take no more? Why was the pathway forward revealed only when my physical strength was at its lowest? Why was the friendly hand extended at the time I needed it most?

I do not have good answers to any of these questions.

What I do know is this revelation uncovered another way of viewing my world and seeing myself.

It was through experiencing the fire of grief that I came to know what it is like to be physically healed – the fearful self transformed to a manful self.

I have no other explanation for the change I experienced on my yacht, of being guided to draw on the embedded strength in the wordless learnings of my childhood, buried deep within me.

From that point on, I knew I would lead my family out of the incapacitating circumstances of Ciara's murder, to be there for them.

No one else could undertake this for me.

I could not crumble in front of Una or Denise. Both are very strong women. Each of us was dealing with our grief in our own way. We were journeying different pathways, striving to find the same destination.

Knowing there is somebody there if needed, someone determined to be strong and walk on with gracious dignity, is a potent healing balm.

I now knew I would do whatever it took to not let my family or myself sink into the shifting quicksands of long-term or deep grief. How to do this was unknown to me before that evening.

I would find pathways.

If my family was to function in the circumstances into which we had been catapulted, I had no choice but to be *man of the house, head of the family,* embracing the age-old, unwritten values and the inescapable responsibilities passed to me.

Rightly or wrongly, this *revelation* became a beacon on the hill for me, to encourage me forward.

When I found myself facing vulnerability, trying to maintain a stance of strength, defiance, perhaps a *bloody* defiance, to overcome the adversity, these deeply buried values came to the fore.

I was guided back to the world, resolved, accepting I was a changed person, the grief now a part of me, confident I would find additional insights or revelations, other pathways, when I explored the other dimensions of grief.

When we have such insights, we have less fear.

The values I speak of cannot be confined to my ethnicity or gender.

They are buried deep in all men who have the good fortune to have been moulded from the clay of a good father.

Can these values be passed from grandfather and father to the daughters of fathers who have no sons?

Unquestionably.

Ciara had them, her sister Denise has them, and she is passing them to her children.

Can comparably powerful values be passed from grandmothers and mothers to daughters, and through them to their children?

Unquestionably.

13
Psychological Impacts and Perfect Imperfection

The mind that opens to a new idea never returns to its original size.

Albert Einstein

When we lose a child, the impacts of grief change us intellectually; this kind of grief is a thief of minds.

Our brain struggles to make any sense of what has happened. There are enormous knowledge gaps that cannot ever be explained; cracks we think can never be repaired, never healed.

Such grief casts a shadow over and limits our imagination. We are unable to see past the suffering that plagues us. At the time, we just need answers for what has happened and how to deal with the debilitating psychological impacts.

My search for rational explanations for Ciara's murder was relentless, continuing day and night, for months and months and months. Why did it happen to me? What had I done, not done, to deserve this?

It was hard to find steppingstones onto which I could safely step when I was confused and bewildered and no answers were forthcoming.

All the thinking and searching I did to ameliorate the psychological impacts of grief provided no immediate pathways. My response: more searching, more reading. Still no answers, no pathways.

Persistent reading and searching for explanations in the grief literature unconsciously kept me isolated from entering the cocoon of my own woundedness, suffering and grief. I remained blind to what teachings about the psychological impacts might be found there. My refusal to face the grief itself was very present. Instead, I only wanted to escape from it.

Such escapism was not the reality of the world I was in. I was caught in a cycle of damaging cognitive distortions, skewed ideas about the altered world I was thrown into.

It is very hard to ask the mind to interpret things differently and think of new solutions when you're trapped by fear, anguish, sadness, grief. Such impeded thinking makes solutions nigh impossible to find.

The raw truth is that sometimes terrible things happen in this life; that is the human condition. My life had changed. I had no choice but to see it for what it was. This was not easy to accept.

The human mind is stubborn. It is not like a chessboard where we can easily move pieces around from one square to the next. Our psychological world is a very resistant part of us and making changes in it isn't easy, nor do changes take place rapidly. Mental constructs, our thoughts – especially irrational ones – can be embedded very deeply. They are rigid and not receptive to being challenged. Changing the way we think requires hard work to break thought patterns we have become attached to, thoughts that appear to be on autopilot, thoughts we have unconsciously absorbed, forming our dominant belief systems.

But it is possible to reconstruct our thoughts. When our irrational thoughts can be identified and confronted, pathways are opened to replace the distortions with more 'realistic' or adaptive thoughts. In early grief, these potentially transformational pathways are dimly lit, vague and in darkness for quite some time.

One morning I was reading and the crucial insight revealed itself: *I would only change my thinking about the psychological impacts if the prospect of not changing it was more of the same pain.*

I did not wish to remain bound to that prospect. Why must we go to the edge of losing something before we recognise its value?

That was the 'light bulb' moment. The insight. The revelation.

Before commencing the healing of the psychological impacts, part of me needed to die, namely, *a dying of my unremitting search for mortal, intellectual explanations for the insanity of what had happened.*

This was incongruous. If I stop searching for answers, how or from where will I find help to move forward, to heal the unremitting psychological impacts?

I trusted in this revelation. Why, I do not know.

I ceased searching for explanations on ways to shake off the nightmare of the psychological impacts from which I was constantly seeking to escape.

This ceasing was not borne of frustration, but of awakening.

The initiation of that action, to stop the searching, was key to finding healing for the psychological impacts.

I let the mystery of the revelation progress at its own pace, trusting it would reveal pathways to reconcile the dilemma of having no answers to my questions about how to ease the continued suffering, yet ceasing the search for them.

No philosophical or theological explanation, no theory about evil can explain the objective evil of Ciara's death. The raw truth is that is the human condition; it is the life we share on this earth.

This less distracted state of mind slowly, but progressively, allowed me to accept that the incessant searching for intellectual answers as to why Ciara was murdered took me away from the psychological impacts of the grief itself, and what they might eventually reveal to me or teach me.

A restoration of calmness came when I gave up wishing that life was other than it was; when I surrendered to the painful truth of what was – no mortal explanations.

In that calmness, I discovered that where suffering lives, so too do *glimpses of new wisdom* and *flashes of deeper truth*, awaiting to emerge to apply balm to the wounds of my mind – to the psychological impacts. It was, paradoxically, this revelation, to *stop* the searching for reasons or explanations in the grief literature, that brought me any peace worth having.

The initiative clearly required of me was to radically change the way I thought about my ardent desire to understand the psychological impacts of my grief. But how?

The insight to initiate action I found in the ancient Japanese philosophy of *wabi-sabi* and the sixteenth-century Japanese art of Kintsugi – a long way from grief literature.

In traditional Japanese aesthetics, *wabi-sabi* is a philosophy of life centred on acceptance of transience and imperfection. It is sometimes described as one of appreciating beauty that is imperfect, impermanent and incomplete, in nature and in life.

Leonard Koren in his book *Wabi-Sabi: For Artists, Designers, Poets and Philosophers* explains: *Wabi-sabi is the beauty of things imperfect, impermanent, and incomplete, the antithesis of our classical Western notion of beauty as something perfect, enduring, and monumental.*

Richard Powell, in his book *Wabi Sabi Simple: Create Beauty, Value Imperfection, Live Deeply*, explains it as: *Wabi-sabi nurtures all that is authentic by acknowledging three simple realities: nothing lasts, nothing is finished, and nothing is perfect.*

Beth Kempton, in her book *Wabi Sabi: Japanese Wisdom for a Perfectly Imperfect Life*, comments: *With roots in Zen and the Way of Tea, wabi sabi teaches you to see beauty in imperfection, appreciate simplicity, and* **accept the transient nature of all things**. *It inspires you to simplify everything and concentrate on what truly matters.*

Adopting the wabi-sabi view of life to better understand the psychological impacts of grief allowed me to acknowledge that the psychological impacts were part of the ever-evolving altered life in which I found myself. They were not going to be 'got rid of', no matter how much searching I did for pathways to do so, or how strongly I sought their excision from me. Whilst pathways to reach this point were at times opaque, not pleasant or easy, they eventually led to a release from my intellectual inertia to a deeper understanding of my grief and, most of all, acceptance of how multifaceted and imperfect our thinking is, and can remain so.

Wabi-sabi thinking provided a tangible release from incessant inquiry, from the darkened cell of an exasperated mind.

Gradually, I learned not to live in a state of constant longing to escape from the psychological impacts. Instead, I discovered a state of contentment. I stopped striving to achieve an unattainable level of perfectionism of intellectual knowledge as to why Ciara was murdered. This knowledge was just not available and never will be.

This sense of contentment continued to be real and has been maintained during difficult times. It is constant and continuing.

I drew further strength from a pragmatic application of the wabi-sabi philosophy: the creative art of Kintsugi. Poetically translated to 'golden joinery', Kintsugi is the art of repairing broken pottery with a tree sap lacquer mixed with powdered gold. Once completed, seams of gold glint in the conspicuous cracks of the ceramic. The cracks were the psychological impacts on me. Like the gaps in my early knowledge, once considered to be unacceptable obstacles to lucid thought, they were no longer the focus of discontent.

A broken piece of pottery is made whole again, and within its gold-filled cracks there is a world of meaning – the art of embracing imperfection.

This type of repair to Japanese pottery is founded on the premise that embracing the imperfections creates a stronger, more beautiful, exquisite piece of art, highlighting the 'scars' as part of the fuller design. It becomes a part of the history of an object, implying the repairs can make things better, the object being transformed to become more valuable than when it was brand new. The Kintsugi approach celebrates each piece's unique history, *emphasising* its fractures, cracks and brokenness, instead of hiding, disguising or spurning them. Kintsugi embraces the faults, the impacts of damage.

Bonnie Kemske in her book *Kintsugi: The Poetic Mend* melds the concepts of grief and Kintsugi beautifully:

> *Kintsugi traces memory, bringing together the moment of destruction and the gold seams of repair through finely honed skills and painstaking, time-consuming labour in the creation of a new pot from the old.* **There is a story to be told with every crack, every chip. This story inevitably leads to kintsugi's greatest strength: an intimate metaphoric narrative of loss and recovery, breakage and restoration, tragedy, and the ability to overcome it.** *A kintsugi repair speaks of individuality and uniqueness,* **fortitude and resilience, and the beauty to be found in survival**. *Kintsugi leads us to a* **respectful and appreciative acceptance of hardship** *and ageing.*

Embracing grief is learning to live with it, not being afraid to show it, instead acknowledging it as part of my cracked self, with gracious dignity.

Repairing and healing thoughts that are broken can create something unique, more resilient and stronger. The healing of the psychological impacts, I believe, created a stronger, more resilient self. I continue living with contentment, alongside my lacquered, golden psychological cracks.

The psychological cracks or woundedness are an undeniable part of me, but are no longer hurtful, deleterious or to be hidden, out of sight. Now, whenever I go through a period that is tough and deeply sorrowful, I know for certain any cracks can be made stronger, more exquisite, a part of the changed me.

The psychological impacts are now integral parts of me, are not going away, and can never be pushed away by escapism into literature or further intellectual rigour.

I still do not know of any academic, psychological or scriptural answers to the backward-looking questions about why Ciara's murderer did what he did. I think of my ceaseless searching differently now than I did before. Then, the cruel lack of answers were intellectual gaps, cracks filled with grief, confusion and pain-filled memories.

Now the gaps remain as just memories, not carrying suffering or misunderstood preconceptions. Instead, they are filled with acceptance and contentment.

The *glimpses of new wisdom* and *flashes of deeper truths* that were revealed when I *stopped* my searching for intellectual explanations in the grief literature occurred over many, many years. The wisdom and truths allowed a view of life through a wabi-sabi lens, casting a continuing, more luminous light onto pathways forward.

Only when I accepted the enduring presence in me of what I most wanted to avoid and get rid of – the psychological impacts – did I experience the beginnings of a welcomed, yet mysterious, kind of healing.

It was not an end to the suffering or grief, but the sense of peace of mind was real and helpful. The two forms of healing (physical and psychological) were working in harmony, assisting and supporting each other.

Those who meditate believe access to the same deeper meaning, wisdom and truth becomes possible. It took a great deal of time to get to a point where I understood these insights and eventually recognised they could be helpful. It was a long, lonely road and contrary to what intuition or common sense led me to expect. Not seeking answers in the world of grief literature manifested knowledge from within, and from an early, oriental philosophy of life.

It is as though my capacity to open to the possibility of living with grief allowed me to grasp the *wisdom* and *truth*, the key to unlocking the door to a healing of the psychological impacts.

I am grateful for being given the insight to stop the incessant, mind-numbing searching for intellectual explanations for Ciara's murder.

There are none.

This healing of the psychological impacts of grief took place at a much slower pace than the physiological rebuilding, but its presence and power is persistent and omnipresent.

With a calmer and wiser mind, I continued to explore the impacts of the other two dimensions (emotional and spiritual), trusting I would again be assisted to find pathways to be further healed.

14
Emotional Impacts and Meditation

No one ever told me that grief felt so like fear.

C.S. Lewis

Our *perceptual* senses – sight, touch, hearing, smell, taste – produce 'maps' of the outside world and transform this external world into mental images or thoughts. In much the same way, our feelings or emotions transform our internal world (the state of our bodies, our sense of wellbeing) into mental images and thoughts.

How we feel, whether our emotions remain placid or erupt, is the result of a continuous conversation between our *feeling* body and our *knowing* mind. The importance of the former is difficult to exaggerate. Not surprisingly, emotions are important contributors to the armature of our personhood, the makeup of our 'self'.

We use words to describe the experiences of *feeling,* but we do not need the mediation of words to *feel*. We don't need words to tell us grief's intensity only increases when it consolidates its grip on our feelings, our emotions. We just know, without being told, and extraordinarily without having to use any of our perceptual senses. That's how distinctive and powerful our emotional makeup is.

The phrase *I think, therefore I am* is an English translation of the Latin phrase *Cogito ergo sum,* first used in 1637 by the French philosopher

Rene Descartes, arguing that our thoughts define who we are, regardless of any other factors.

I suggest the dictum *I feel, therefore I am* is just as valid as Descartes' *I think, therefore I am.*

Feeling need not be the enemy of thought or reason, but an indispensable collaborator.

This is the position I adopted. Both dictums could be of legitimate and genuine help, as I sought to better understand the emotional impacts of grief. There was no need for me to spend time trying to untangle the much published philosophical and academic debates on the correctness or influence of one dictum over the other. It was clear to me the cognitive part of my brain could only function properly when the emotional turmoil in my brain abated.

Those who have experienced intense grief well know of the interconnectedness between the psychological and emotional impacts. Whether a *feeling* of unbearable sadness is generated in our mind or in our heart, or partly in each, is irrelevant. We certainly *feel* its dead weight and hurt, regardless of its birthplace.

Every emotional impact we feel is influenced by our thoughts. The gateway to a better understanding of the emotional impacts of my grief was through my thoughts, especially the frequently occurring ones, the ones surfacing unconsciously, unquestionably contributing to the feelings of sadness, loneliness, fear, helplessness and so on.

When trying to identify the thoughts underlying the emotional impacts of my grief, I quickly realised I could not even write a shortlist. I commenced by scribbling simple notes on the most frequently occurring thoughts that came into my head; thoughts that always hurt and frightened me; thoughts I pushed away as soon as they arrived. These scribblings formed an initial shortlist.

When alone or unable to sleep, I repetitively, unconsciously returned to the same thought pattern, the same mental images – the *sadness of the past* and the *fear of the future*, both of which subconsciously recreated and generally made worse the emotional impacts of my grief.

I felt as if I was trapped inside the confines of the past, which I wanted to run from, and the fear of the future, which I did not want to face, with no time given to any thought of the *present*.

I felt I was in a dark storehouse, brimming with thoughts that were trapping me in an emotionally barren world.

These early scribblings revealed that light had to illuminate that storehouse if I wished to experience any feeling of contentment in the present.

I have never formally studied or practised meditation, but I was drawn to the concept of a mantra, as a way to help stop or at least decrease the frequency and intensity of the negative recurring thought patterns that were impacting how I felt.

I tried a few different words and very short phrases from Buddhist readings as mantras, but these were not helpful for me.

My thoughts kept returning to the injustice of losing Ciara (the past) and to the picture of life without her (the future). Trying to focus on the present moment was impossible. I knew I was consciously running from it, too, because it held the essence of my grief – the terrible circumstances in which Ciara died. These thoughts and images were too hard to face.

The *present moment* is central to all literature on meditation. A concentration on breathing is also a dominant component of meditation practices. The concept of the present moment was vague, tenuous, elusive, confronting. It was not only hard to face, but it was also being crowded out by the sad past and frightening future thoughts.

To break this impasse, I decided to construct a personal mantra, one that would acknowledge the parity and legitimacy of all three categories of thought.

A mantra need not be confined to a single word. It can be a few words with the same purpose – to calm my mind and focus my intention. The word 'mantra' is derived from two Sanskrit word, *tra* (tool) and *manas* (mind) – a tool for the mind that might help me focus thought and find a pathway to the present moment, to a healing of the emotional impacts.

After countless false starts, I wrote the following mantra:

The past is the past; the future is the future. Both are part of me. I can change neither. I can only influence the present, which is part of me, too. Sit quietly in its still waters, just breathing.

A little long perhaps, but it made sense for me. I imagined myself alone, sitting in a small pool of tepid, crystal-clear water on a windless beach, eyes closed, breathing gently, endeavouring to be as calm as I could.

I had initiated action to finding a pathway and as I persevered, I became more aware of my breathing, as I whispered the words of the mantra.

After two or three months of sporadic success, the more aware I became of my breathing, the more comfortable I was to think of the present and endeavour to stay in the *present moment*, focusing on not having it crowded out by thoughts of past and future.

A concentration on exhaling at a slower pace than inhaling helped me to stop floating away from being in the present moment. For the first time, I understood the inseparability of my thoughts of the past, present and future, as well as how my life was being altered, forever, by all three – not individually, but concurrently.

The past would not be pushed into some dark corner, to be run away from and forgotten. The future would not be cast beyond the horizon of my mind, in the hope it would remain hidden.

To find a healing of the emotional impacts, the past and the future had to cease being my enemies; the trauma had to be faced in the present moment, not shut out.

I experienced a degree of relief and felt I could live with all three. Thoughts of the past and the future did not instantaneously fade away, but they lost their muscle to repetitively inflict sadness and fear. I found narrow pathways on which small steps could be taken towards spending time in the present moment.

Many times I was enticed to reject all efforts to persist with thoughts of the present moment; it held the essence of my grief.

Leonard Cohen in his song *Anthem* sings: *Do not dwell on what is past, or what is yet to be...there is a crack, there is a crack in everything, that's how the light gets in.*

A crack opened for me between the past and the future, filling me with more courage that I was going to be safe, that light would shine into the dark storehouse.

As I became more adept at focusing attention on the present moment, I was less and less torn away by thoughts of the past and future. Instead of trying to fend off the emotional impacts of my grief, I was able to sit with them, increasingly accepting they were now part of me.

I could not alter the way Ciara was murdered or do anything to soften her last frightening moments. These thoughts and the images I viewed in the autopsy report are ingrained in my mind, and in my heart. Not erasable, I have learned to sit with them.

The emotional impacts were being tempered, forged and healed, and were integral elements of who I had become.

The increased feelings of peace, less heartbrokenness and serenity guided me to not fight against, but instead hold on to, the suffering of the past and the fear of the future as well as experiencing a new contentment in the present moment.

The presence of all three coexisted in the altered self. They no longer thrashed around in that dark storehouse, trapped in the cauldron of the emotional impacts of my grief.

The temptation to give up was ever present, and I suspect no person in grief is spared this. The words attributed to Confucius are apt: *It does not matter how slowly you go so long as you do not stop*.

If my mind started to drift to either the past or the future, I imagined myself gently lowering a little further into the tepid, still, clear waters of the present moment, to its sense of calmness. Another small step forward; I was happy with moment-to-moment progress.

I stayed with my mantra, trusting the tide would continue to turn. It did.

I experienced a new state of mind, revealing a more balanced and congenial relationship between the three elements of thought, recognising my thoughts of the past and future for what they were – just thoughts, coming and going like wavelets on the beach. I sat in the increasingly tranquil waters of the present, at peace with my disquiet, alone with my thoughts, without judgement, with a sense of *contentment*.

This enriched my awareness and attentiveness to lessen uninvited rumination, nurture my wellbeing, enhance self-insight and experience increased lucidity of thought.

Without anger, guilt or fear, I tapped into the state of contentment, the manifested healing of the emotional impacts.

I had turned towards my grief and I was understanding it.

The words of Buddhist monk Claude Anshin Thomas, *Suffering is not my enemy*, now make more sense to me.

The emotional bleeding stopped and some more of the grief was healed.

There remained a final dimension – the spiritual dimension.

15
Spiritual Impacts and Transcendence

Gratitude bestows reverence, allowing us to encounter everyday epiphanies, those transcendent moments of awe that change forever how we experience the world.

John Milton

Before addressing the spiritual impacts, I will summarise the confusion I experienced about the place of God in all this. My strongest anger and interrogations were directed towards the God I believed in. I fired at Him the most agonising questions from my wounded, angry soul, to which there were no answers.

All I seemed to know was an absconded or vanished God.

On reflection, fixation on such questions can only be born of anger.

Distinct from the physical exhaustion, the psychological confusion and emotional heartbrokenness, staring at me was the search for healing of the most difficult impacts of all, the spiritual ones.

My Catholic faith offered no protection against suffering, nor did it offer any insurance against the thoughts of spiritual doubt and apparent betrayal. I could not fit the pieces together.

All conversations with God were 'one way'. I doubted if He was even present and if He was, at best, it was a vague, vexing presence. Finding prayerful words was impossible.

It is always hard to hear another when you are angry with them and have doubts about their presence. What if God had been talking to me all along, but just in whispers I didn't hear?

The spiritual impacts of grief are unfathomable, their upheaval unsettling. Trying to make sense of the senseless is spiritually demanding work, impenetrable to any rational understanding.

Writing about the impacts of this dimension of grief was akin to trying to capture a bubble – the closer I got to it, the further the wind blew it away from me.

Describing in credible words any relief from the spiritual impacts is testing for a Christian, a believer. Questions surrounding these impacts bring added layers of complexity and struggle to believing parents, no matter which belief system they adhere to.

Nonbelievers do not have to grapple with these questions. For them, there is no Higher Being. Believers do have to grapple with them. I am a Christian, a believer.

My grapple with the spiritual impacts was fundamentally a searching for answers to the otherworldly questions about how a just and loving God could allow Ciara to be murdered, so brutally, and allow me to suffer such consequential grief.

Each time I thought I was getting close to some revelation, some insight, some answers to my questions, like the bubble they drifted further away. I read and searched the literature on grief and spirituality. However, the more I sought explanations for the otherworldly questions, the more despondent I became of finding any insights or revelations.

I reached a point where I was left with no choice but to acknowledge that *nobody really knows* if universal beliefs, such as divine caring, the goodness of God, unconditional love by God, trusting in God, finding a sacred meaning in suffering and the like, *are true or not*.

Worldly legitimacy of these kinds of spiritual belief are not to be found in grief or ecclesiastical literature, or in religious rituals. Constantly chasing evidence of, or truth in, such universal beliefs when physically, psychologically and emotionally drained by grief is but a diversion of precious energy.

I ceased searching for explanations, remaining unaided, naked in a spiritual desert.

The unanswered questions continued to keep me awake at night, fatigued, confused, spiritually abandoned, my belief in God crushed, my faith severely tested, with zero feeling that the God I had believed in for so many years was even present in my life when I needed Him most or would ever be present again. I ceased attending Mass.

I was at another threshold, having no option but to concede there were no earthly answers or religious remedies to understand and heal these spiritual impacts.

I clearly remember the moment of conceding, of 'giving in'.

When I did, a pathway forward revealed itself, in unexpected circumstances.

It happened serendipitously. Being open to serendipity is important to grief healing. It cannot be forced but we can be open to it.

I was on my boat, *Calypso V*, having a tough time spiritually, continually arguing with God about his injustice, his absence, getting no answers, feeling I was going under, with no one to hear me, no one to turn to.

From some distant past, probably my childhood catechism classes, I remembered the words: *Ask and it will be given to you; seek and you will find; knock and the door will be opened to you.*

I had not recalled or spoken these words for over forty-five years.

Discovered in a miniature moment from something larger inside me, a distilled essence and lucidity of thought emerged.

It was a revelation, a recognition that another way was being offered, inviting me to a healing from the impacts in this spiritual dimension.

I simply thought, perhaps prayed: *God, I do not understand why you let this happen. It is all too much for me. I am handing this whole grief thing over to you. I am asking. Please, please take it from me.*

I could not say the words aloud, crying had choked my throat, stifled my voice. I whispered them.

I accepted His invitation and handed my grief over to Him, beseeching that it be lifted from me, desperately trying not to confuse listening for really hearing.

A clarity of thought unveiled itself. It was illogical, contradictory, remarkable; a gracious moment when I recognised it.

God was *not absent* when Ciara was killed, and he was not absent when I was arguing with him. *He was present.*

The sense of His presence, on my boat that evening, was unmistakable, tangible, a forcefield of presence.

I am unsure I can articulate it, other than that it was a sense of *connectedness, togetherness, transcendence*. There is a great deficit in our language to describe a connection between grief and this forcefield of presence. I cautiously recognise there are mysteries in life.

Meister Eckhart is insightful: *There's a place in the soul where you've never been wounded.*

Who knows what unforeseen connections occur at the soul/spirit level and how companionship with the soul happens? Two metaphors may help.

Connectedness to nature

The *connectedness* and *togetherness* I experienced that evening was akin to, but stronger than, the *connectedness to nature* and *togetherness with my boat* I experience when I go to sea, especially when sailing alone.

There, I discover solitude and surprise. My boat makes deeply contented sounds as she reverentially bows to her own sea gods. A steady, kind wind embraces her sails. Together we slip mile after mile over a languid ocean. The waves doff their small whitecaps and ripple and rhythm against her hull. A miniature, inimitable rainbow appears, dancing on her bow wave. I will never see it again.

When fortunate, I am accompanied by a pod of dolphins with their leaping, splashing joy; they play around, then swim rhythmically to the horizon, leaving behind the soft sound of the breathing of the sea and stillness. Both embrace my mind and heart. I know then my boat's kind soul is present.

This is a place and time where the outer quietude prevails over the inner restiveness and leads to a private silence.

A growing trust in the inner voice is nurtured. It calls me to untie myself from the anxieties of daily life and entrust myself to the familiar *connectedness* I have been invited to, by my friend, nature.

The diaphanous mystery of transcendence to another world, a deeper level, is uncovered.

My senses have been awakened; the ephemerality of my *connectedness* to nature, *togetherness* with my boat, have manifested themselves.

Music's power of transcendence

Michelangelo was thought to have said, *Music is capable of touching the deeper levels of one's being.*

Ludwig van Beethoven said, *Music is the mediator between the spiritual and the sensual life.*

Martin Luther suggested, *Beautiful music is the art of the prophets that can calm the agitations of the soul; it is one of the most magnificent and delightful presents God has given us.*

Tolstoy calls music, *the shorthand of emotion.*

English novelist Arnold Bennett wrote, *Its language is a language which the soul alone understands but which the soul can never translate.*

Blogger Elizabeth Trites says, *Music is one of the most deeply and widely established ways for people to transcend their daily lives.*

Music opens parts of my soul. It is what we would like language to be.

What makes a cello sound like the cry of the human voice, saddened by death or loss? Why does some music transport us to memories of places and people, decades ago and thousands of kilometres away? Why do we remember music that soothes sadness, and even if the sadness does not lift entirely, somehow the music helps us live with it? Pieces in our personal music playlists can lift us to ecstasy.

Why do we 'soften and surrender to' the pathos in some music?

I do, when I listen to music like: *Claire de Lune* by Claude Debussy; *Come, Sweet Death* by Johann Sebastian Bach; *Hallelujah* by Leonard Cohen; *Tears in Heaven* by Eric Clapton; *Every Breath You Take* by The Police; *The Sounds of Silence* by Simon and Garfunkel.

Why do we want to shake our heads, play air violins, beat rhythm with imaginary drumsticks, tap our toes, feel like dancing, smile and be happy when we listen to Mozart's *Sonata No. 17 in C; The Marriage of Figaro* by Mozart; *Hoe Down* by Copland; *Dancing Queen* by Abba; *Walking on Sunshine* by Katrina and the Waves?

The movie *Alive Inside* is a truly inspirational documentary on the healing power of music in patients suffering from Alzheimer's disease. Most people cry and are uplifted when they watch it.

Music takes our mind 'out' of our environment, stimulates unanticipated changes of mood, unlocks richer levels of inner companionship, stirs the deepest of buried emotions and puts time on hold. Soft, relaxing music instils in me the same harmonious concord I mysteriously experience on my boat, in the wind and water, in nature. It is impossible to find the best words to describe what is happening.

A good friend of mine who is trained in classical music and is an international orchestral player says: *At first, I 'absorb' the music, until it reaches a place in my inner self, when the music soon totally absorbs me, and transports me to places where its extraordinary power evokes emotions, as if an inner connection had been established between the music and my spirit.*

He likens a great musical performance or experience to being a solo glider soaring on a powerful thermal (the music) and letting it transport him wherever it will to experience an uplifting transcendental symbiosis between his spirit and the music. Nobody else is there, nothing distracts from the moment.

When we listen to music, its innate power affects our body, mind, heart and spirit. This power is invisible. It is embedded in the music. We can hear it, there is no doubting its presence and transcendent potency. We hear the music but can neither grasp nor hold the embodied transcendence. Perhaps it has been created in the ignited soul of the conductor of the orchestra.

Friedrich Nietzsche could partially illustrate this transcending power of music with these words:

> *God has given us music so that above all it can lead us upwards. Music unites all qualities: it can exalt us, divert us, cheer us up, or break the hardest of hearts with the softest of its melancholy tones. But its principal task is* **to lead our thoughts to higher things**, *to elevate, even to make us tremble...The musical art often speaks in sounds more penetrating than the words of poetry and* **takes hold of the most hidden crevices of the heart**...*Song elevates*

our being and leads us to the good and the true. If, however, music serves only as a diversion or as a kind of vain ostentation it is sinful and harmful.

Many times whilst writing this book, when the words would not come, I put 'down my pen', pushed the keyboard aside, and turned to music. That always helped.

Music's mysterious powers help me *transcend* and *connect* me to the mind places it takes me to, just like my boat and me *together connect* me to nature and the sea. There is a truthfulness and integrity in an *other-worldly presence,* like the transcendent force in nature and music.

What caused me to experience much the same form of *connectedness, togetherness* and *transcendence* when I handed over my suffering that evening, on *Calypso V*?

In stark terms, it came down to me having to face and answer the question: *Do I believe in a God or do I not?* If I do not, my choice was to remain entrapped on the threshold: no crossing, no manifestation, no healing.

If this continued to be my position, I had to give up on God.

I was not going to do that.

I have no explanation why it was only then I thought the unthinkable, and quietly whispered the ineffable.

God:

had nothing to do with Ciara's murder

> whilst I thought He was always absent, He was present
>
> is not responsible for or associated with evil in this world
>
> will not intervene in the natural order of things in this life
>
> will not influence an individual's free will or choice to do good or evil
>
> accepts that someone chose to do evil and murder Ciara, and
>
> feels the woundedness of this wrongdoing, and just as much as it hurt me, it hurt Him.

He was a parent, too. His child was crucified.

Did I feel any presence of some surreal deity, goddess or god when whispering these words?

Yes, but again I don't have the right words to describe it. Perhaps there are no words.

I just thought I had put in the work trying to fathom the spiritual impacts of grief, and when the conditions were right, believed the pathways would reveal themselves.

Was it a spiritual awakening or epiphany? I do not think it was. I prefer to think of it as another *manifestation*. Rather than a sudden epiphany or awakening, the wavelets of this manifestation can be recognised better with hindsight, yet can be traced back to that conceding, that invitation, that single event at that point in time. The shift in thinking is best described as gradual, consistent and continuing. There is wisdom in this hindsight.

The overwhelming thought I had that evening was that I was going to be looked after, things were going to be alright. It was a significant shift for me. From that point, I knew I had a pathway towards healing the spiritual impacts of my grief. Perhaps utter vulnerability is not only a prerequisite for healing the spiritual impacts but may even be transformative.

The matter between God and me was closed that evening.

I can only account for the *enlightenment of understanding* that came to me that evening regarding my doubts about God's absence and the one-sided arguments I had with Him as coming from a source outside me.

Boris Pasternak, author of *Doctor Zhivago*, said: *When a great moment knocks on the door of your life, it is often no louder than the beating of your heart, and it is very easy to miss it.*

The person who left the aft cabin that evening was not the same person who entered it. Nothing has ever felt clearer.

A quality of light that is very precious progressively returned to the shadowy spiritual world I had been living in. This manifestation did not conflict with those revealed for a better understanding of the physical, psychological and emotional impacts; it helped shore them up.

It is what we do with the revelation that matters. That is the manifestation.

To this day, I am comfortable with how the *spiritual enlightenment* occurred. The earlier questions about God which were filled with obliviousness, frustration, disbelief and anger gradually ebbed away.

Ciara's murder and its resultant suffering and grief could easily have turned me against the spirituality and belief in the sacred I held.

It didn't.

From deep in each dimension of grief, manifestations occurred:

> mental toughness
>
> restored physical strength
>
> implacable determination
>
> greater courage
>
> glimpses of wisdom
>
> flashes of deeper truth
>
> entry into the present moment, and the past, present and future thoughts accepted for what they were – just thoughts, their potency to continue to wound removed
>
> contentment
>
> enlightenment of understanding.

Together, these were the threads that wove the tapestry of the healings of the totality of impacts, allowing grief to be understood, diminished and integrated into me.

I felt I had crossed all thresholds, hopefully honourably.

This last crossing healed the patterns of destructive repetitious thoughts that had me shackled, and from that threshold I moved forward onto new ground, unshackled, where I could face, not fear or try to escape from, what I had been through.

I live peacefully with that.

The *enlightenment of understanding* I experienced had nothing to do with the trappings of church life, religion or other earthly symbolisms of the mysterious force sustaining life. To arrive at this understanding I accept, without condition, that someone, some force somewhere – for me, God – understood my suffering and grief.

As Ciara's father, whilst I played a very small part in her creation, there also was a greater mysterious force present at conception. That ultimate Creator of life knows what I am enduring. A part of His creation died, too, when Ciara was murdered. This is someone to whom I can turn and be understood by, though very frequently not receive answers to my questions.

Whilst spiritual comfort was absent when I showed anguish, anger and doubt, God was present. I was just too angry and upset to recognise Him. Healing from the spiritual impacts of grief requires a big leap in faith.

I took it.

I am glad I did.

Many times my faith failed to provide any protection from the woundedness and suffering. But in the end, when I needed it most, it came to the forefront and provided the pathway to a healing of the spiritual impacts.

My life today goes on. I try to live life to the fullest, each day.

I cannot refute it reflects the loss of Ciara.

She is now not of this life and will remain 'out there'. What 'out there' looks like or means and what will happen there, I do not understand.

That is acceptable.

What has emerged from Ciara's murder is a wisdom that has little to do with theological study, dogma or religious rituals. It has a great deal to do with healings that manifested themselves as I faced the impacts of the four dimensions of grief. These healings, in their totality, were a spiritual liberation, allowing me to move forward.

16
Moving Forward from Grief Requires Learning to Live with Grief

Every time we make the decision to love someone,
we open ourselves to great suffering.

Henri J.M. Nouwen

Grief is an unwanted inhabitant in every parent who has lost a child. Its presence is protected by the absence of the lost child. It insists on only being carried, lived with and not being dumped behind as if it becomes a 'nothing' after a certain period.

Immediately after Ciara's murder, grief was firmly in control. There was no option but to endure it. I had no idea this would happen. Acute grief has an isolation, an apparent intellect of its own and an inescapable reality.

I could not hide from it. Each time I tried, it found me.

It was not something I could just pass through, hoping to come out the same person on the other side. There is no other side, certainly not one the same as it was before. Always, a sinister chameleon, grief's ghostly hands, in the early days kept drawing me back to the place where suffering resided, shackling me to its perpetuity of presence.

Learning to live with grief was a mixture of surrender and resistance, of vulnerability, of exposure of my own frailty, and of trust, whilst remaining defiant and not giving in to its crushing weight, especially in prolonged periods of stasis.

It exposed the raw truth, time after time, that I had no real control over my life, instead having to accept the powerlessness.

The stark choice every parent faces is to surrender to their grief whilst trying to understand it, do the best they can to live through it, then learn to live with it, or continue to resist its potency, with all the will and strength they can muster.

The choice at first appears binary.

It does not necessarily have to be a dichotomous choice, one or the other.

At times, I had no option but to surrender to grief. Paradoxically, I refused to take it lying down; it was not going to get the better of me. I walked between defiance and surrender, between comfort and discomfort. This mix kept the small flame of hope burning inside me.

Christine Valters Paintner in her book *Earth – Our Original Monastery* articulates this balance exquisitely: *We often learn the most about ourselves by dancing on those edge places between comfort and discomfort, with gentleness.*

I stayed on these edge places, dancing with gentleness. Not as a broken person, but a defiant person, who surrendered when no other option was obvious. With increasing *mental toughness* and *implacable determination*, I kept moving forward, alongside grief, finding little shards of light, accepting my altered life. The person I was before Ciara's murder had gone, forever.

Samira Thomas in her essay 'In praise of patience' states: *From this landscape, I take the lesson that I* ***need not be who I once was****, that I may hold my scars and my joy simultaneously. I* ***need not choose between bending or breaking*** *but that, through patience, I may be transfigured* .

Living with grief was and is a continual discovery of new edge places connecting my life before Ciara's murder to my life now, and inevitably to what it is still to be.

Revisiting life before her murder is now less sad, less distressing, and I do not fear where I am or the life still to come. It is much better because it is free of the kind of suffering that accompanies holding on to the notion that grief is a problem to be fixed.

Grief from the loss of a child cannot be *fixed*.

It can be *lived with* in dignity and resilience in the altered life.

PART III

17
Is Forgiveness Necessary for a Sense of Peace?

Forgiveness is not about letting someone off the hook for their actions, but freeing ourselves of negative thoughts that bind us to them.

Satsuki Shibuya

Like most aspects of grief, the answer to this question is not straightforward. The two conventional options on forgiveness are (1) hold on to grief, anger, resentment and even thoughts of revenge, or (2) embrace forgiveness and 'move forward with life'.

The opinion repeatedly given to me was, if I don't forgive, I might be the one who ends up paying the biggest price, as forgiveness is a prerequisite for finding any kind of peace that will allow me to move on with life. Friends and colleagues contended that forgiveness would play an important part in releasing me from the grips of the past. It would help me to process grief and see life in a different way, intimating my future life was greater than the grief.

Advice in the literature from health professionals, psychologists and grief counsellors predominantly supports this view, asserting there is a moral imperative to forgive, as forgiveness can be a force of healing.

Dr Tyler VanderWeele, co-director of the Initiative on Health, Religion, and Spirituality at the Harvard T.H. Chan School of Public Health states:

Forgiving a person who has wronged you is never easy but dwelling on those events and reliving them over and over can fill your mind with negative thoughts and suppressed anger...***When you learn to forgive, you are no longer trapped by the past actions of others and can finally feel free.***

An article by The Johns Hopkins Hospital states:

> *There is an enormous physical burden to being hurt and disappointed. Chronic anger puts you into a fight-or-flight mode, which results in numerous changes in heart rate, blood pressure and immune response. Those changes, then, increase the risk of depression, heart disease and diabetes, among other conditions.* **Forgiveness, however, calms stress levels, leading to improved health.**

Wendy Salazar in the online article 'Coping with grief: why forgiveness matters so much', states: ***Our psychological health therefore depends on our ability to forgive others*** .

Nola Metz-Allan in 'The impact of forgiveness on healing and grief' states: *In forgiveness we are choosing a new thought, we are choosing to be compassionate towards ourselves, and it is here that the healing is fostered.*

How useful is this kind of advice to parents who has experienced the greatest loss of all – that of their child? Can they ever forget the death of their child? Is forgiveness necessary for forgetting and moving forward?

Christians believe in a God who forgives the wrongs of people, but our human nature makes it extremely difficult for us to do this.

At least it did and does for me.

Have I forgiven or will I ever forgive the person who murdered Ciara? No.

Have I forgotten or will I ever forget the horrendous fatal wounds inflicted by him on Ciara? No.

I did not follow the prevailing advice from health professionals, counsellors and spiritual one-liners, which stressed that forgiving and forgetting were prerequisites to learning to live alongside grief.

I have moved into a new chapter in my life. I am at peace with myself. The sting of the early grief has greatly diminished, not gone. I am where I am, without feeling any obligation to forgive the perpetrator.

As I mentioned at the outset, the answer is not a straightforward one.

After reading much of the professional literature on forgiveness and listening to the advice offered by close friends and colleagues, I concluded that this kind of 'guidance' was not helpful for me.

Much of it I found offensive, especially that suggesting if I did not forgive the person who murdered Ciara, I would be constantly dwelling on her. It would keep me emotionally bogged down in the injustice and trauma. I would be consumed by negative attitudes and in danger of becoming a permanent victim and remain overwhelmed with thoughts of retribution. I would have to live with the constant tension of not being able to forgive myself for not forgiving the person who committed the evilest act I could conceive of.

Yet, if I forgive, it brings a form of legitimacy to the evil of her murder and attempts to assuage the horror of her death. Her murder was, is and always will be terrible.

This conundrum is not perplexing. It is offensive.

My initial anger and newfound *mental toughness, restored strength, determination* and *courage* had a raw power that (1) beneficially underpinned my confidence to deal with the world I had been catapulted into; (2) strengthened my will to do all in my power to find the person responsible for Ciara's murder; and (3) helped me lead my family with grace, and not become a victim.

Owning and not being ashamed of this healthy anger is non-harmful. It was productive and good for keeping my self-respect and dignity.

The early advice to embrace forgiveness is simply unsympathetic to the very suffering I experienced for years. Forgiveness was not a necessary panacea to heal that suffering. It held out the bogus promise that if I forgave, I could forget, leave the past hidden and move into a new world of non-suffering, without grief.

This view of the world of grief is absurd. It is a falsity.

For some individuals, concentrating on forgiveness may be beneficial and act as a catalyst for healing, but I suggest the positive effects of forgiveness can only help healing if an individual chooses this path and believes in its reported potency. That was not the path I chose.

Fortunately, I was given the wisdom to decide I could live quite easily with myself without having to forgive Ciara's murderer. He is not deserving of forgiveness. This is but a simple truth.

Forgiving him is not important to my wellbeing, state of peace or contentment. I harbour no feelings of hatred or revenge towards him. He is in prison, with a minimum parole period of forty years. It is unlikely he will ever be released, and he will most likely die in prison.

As I worked through grief, I discovered the things that brought rays of peace and contentment into my life, allowing the natural process of grieving to happen at its own pace. My best contribution to that process was to get rid of barriers that got in the way. This included the false notion that I had to forgive the murderer. Once I got rid of this and similar useless notions, the grieving and healing took their natural course.

How I feel about forgiveness is how I feel, and no one can impose something different on me.

My heart is my own.

My mind is my own.

My spirit is my own.

My soul is my own.

My continuing journey to increasing peace and contentment is my own.

I continue to live with the remaining grief from the worst trauma possible, without guilt, without any sense of having to forgive the person who murdered my daughter.

I respect grieving parents who hold different views on the question of forgiveness being a precondition for peace.

None of us can claim to be a sage on grief.

18
Closure – Is this Anything More than a Cliché?

Creatures made of clay with porous skin and porous minds are quite incapable of the hermetic sealing that the strategy of 'closure' seems to imply.

John O'Donohue

Grief from the loss of a child is not a predetermined journey with a neatly packaged 'closing' or end. Conceiving of grief as living with ongoing suffering, without sooner or later finding respite, goes against all our basic instincts. I, like everyone else, was born to be suffering-averse.

I have lost track of the number of people who have asked me if the arrest, trial, conviction and sentencing of the person who murdered Ciara brought *closure*, and allowed me to 'move on with life', 'recover' from grief. Closure of 'what' or move on to 'where'?

When I ask these people what they mean by *closure* they generally refer to the police case being 'closed' and positing I should be able to 'pick myself up' and get back to what they commonly called 'normal living'.

For me, there is no such experience or state of mind as *closure*. The concept is illogical, ludicrous.

If I entertain the possibility of *closure*, it forces me to hold on to beliefs like *I'm over it; I have moved on; I have forgotten about Ciara; I am getting on with life; grief is behind me; there are no more memories; there is no more sadness on birthdays or anniversaries* – an impossibility, unless *closure* equates to total amnesia and I become an amnesiac.

If, on the other hand, the ongoing grief is of a kind I have learned to live reasonably comfortably with, *closure* is less obligatory. Being comfortable with grief permits me to continue to love Ciara, *despite* her physical absence, in a different way, without despair.

Albert Camus, in his book *The Sea Close By,* says: *Those who love and are separated can live in grief; but this is not despair: they know that love exists.*

I could never conceive of my continued love for Ciara diminishing over time or somehow being 'closed'.

The notion of my love of her 'closing down', at some time in the future, is anathema to me. It is an affront and is disrespectful. Love and grief are intertwined, and any sense of a disconnection is an illusion. The concept of *closure* distorts grieving, at least the kind I describe in this book. *Closure* also forces out the deeply healing facet of my continued love for my daughter.

I grieve because Ciara was ripped away from me, causing extraordinary suffering.

The covenant of death and life is the terrible beauty of integrated grief.

Grieving is not about a desperate search for *closure*.

Finding healing for the impacts of grief, yes. This is a totally separate concept and is not about an imaginary endpoint.

I don't need some mythical state of mind called *closure* to heal the impacts that hurt from any of the four dimensions of grief. *Closure* is an artificial concept used by people who wish to have just a conversation about loss and grief, and mostly who have never known intense grief.

Closure, presented in stark black and white, seduces, but has no depth or majesty. It just crystallises the fault lines it promises to repair, grinding to a halt the day-to-day work of honest dealing with grief.

This black and white view is not the reality of life for anyone in grief.

Through photography I know the skill and art of reading light – its quality, type, intensity and its angle and direction. This helps me discern how light will affect the image I am wishing to make. Artists use the same play of light, the melding of shadows and light, especially to create plaintive paintings.

Shadows play a more important role in shaping light, crafting drama, establishing mood, especially rendering depth, capturing the soul of the subject, as well as a kind of melancholic beauty. A knowledge of this interplay is essential for photographers and artists. It is the shadows and the light interwoven, harmonising, each revealing the beauty and mystery in the other.

It is the shadow symbolism in such photographs and paintings that unveils authenticity and beauty in the unknown.

The folds in the clothing and the enigmatic smile in the *Mona Lisa* painting are the archetype of this composite.

Similarly, it's the composite of sadness and contentment that brings depth and character to a parent living with grief.

To journey the shadowland of grief, it was necessary for me to find pathways to live with both grief and my ongoing love for Ciara.

It is the intertwining of grief and love that brings freedom.

It is the freedom grieving parents need, not the falsity of *closure*.

19
'Recovery' from the Loss of a Child – Is this Possible?

You can't go back and change the beginning, but you can start where you are and change the ending.

C.S. Lewis

From a medical perspective, some form of 'healing' should precede *recovery*. When describing the four dimensions of grief, and their associated impacts, I concluded that healing of these impacts was an antecedent to *any sense of peace worth having.*

Is this *sense of peace* the same as *recovery*?

Having arrived at the view on *closure* in the last chapter, I do not have to wonder if there is any correlation between *recovery* and the deceptive concept of *closure*. There isn't any.

What do we mean by *recovery*? A return to *normal living*?

Does *recovery* mean we are 'freed' from grief?

To be understood, grief must not be recoiled against; rather it must be accepted, unconditionally. It becomes an irrefutable part of every grieving parent. Acceptance of this can provide pathways to a new *sense of peace*, a place of *contentment*, whilst still living with diminished grief. This is at first counterintuitive and not quickly or easily grasped by those who have not experienced intense grief.

An analogy may assist.

If a person suffers a significant loss of hearing in both ears, their life is divided into two distinct parts: 'life with hearing' and 'life without hearing'. Once lost, there is no possibility of the lost hearing being restored or healing itself; the hearing will never naturally experience a state of *recovery*.

The person has been 'wounded' and the loss of hearing remains a part of them. No matter how strongly they wish the lost hearing to *recover*, it is not going to happen. Their ability to partake fully in conversations with friends in a busy restaurant or with colleagues in business meetings, or hear beautiful music as they once did, has changed, forever.

The loss of hearing is now an irrefutable part of that person. They cannot ever recover the actual loss. They must accept it. There are no benefits to be gained by fighting against the loss. The miracle of modern hearing aids can assist them to hear again but the actual loss has not changed. The loss itself has not *recovered*. There is no such thing as a *recovery* from hearing loss. Accepting the loss (and the inconvenience of wearing hearing aids) permits them to live with a different sense of joy at being able to hear, albeit differently, again.

Similarly, it is only through an unquestionable acceptance and genuine understanding of the impacts of grief that we can truly know and feel the opposites – contentment alongside the enduring, diminished grief.

Can I envisage a time in the future when the grief will disappear – I will be finally at peace? This is not possible, no more than a loss of hearing will restore itself.

For me, *recovery* is not a precondition for peace or contentment. Grief is now part of me. I have learned to form a transparent relationship with it, neither denying nor rejecting it and, more importantly, not affixing to its negative aspects. It is not anchoring me, imprisoning me in cycles of sadness, which it would if I fought against it, denied its existence, or had not done the work described in earlier chapters.

The healings and manifestations outlined earlier allow me to live in a different relationship with grief so that it does not continue to negatively dominate my thoughts or feelings. This transparent relationship opens me to newfound insights into the nature and meaning of grief itself.

I learned to move in the direction of living alongside grief, trusting that I must let go of any preconceptions, prejudices and beliefs I had about the nature of it. Only then could the truth of grief surface, and I could see it for what it is and what it had done – it has redefined the core of who I am, in ways I had not expected.

When grappling with possible pathways to less sadness, what became more important was not what I did, but more frequently what I had to stop doing.

I had to stop thinking in habitual ways, stop trying to shake off the sadness, stop trying to run away from grief and instead think about what it might teach me.

My elemental 'core' was being irrevocably transformed.

If I had to keep wondering if I would ever *recover*, I would find this to be distinctly unhelpful.

Grief is not my enemy.

I do not believe a parent ever recovers from the loss of their child, but they can be healed to live well with the altered person they have become.

They can find purpose again, without being weighed down, waiting for some mythical day to arrive when they will be fully *recovered*. No such day will ever arrive.

Grief is a universal experience but each parent's healing, their journey through grief, is unique to them. It is also a lifelong journey that does not end, perhaps for any parent. We adjust and find new pathways to carry the weight – for our families, for ourselves.

Thus, the answer to the original question depends on what we mean by *recovery*.

If *recovery* is to mean I return to be the same person I was before Ciara's murder, in order for this to happen I would have to somehow neatly package and forget her loss, 'move on' with my life, and emerge on the other side of grief pretty much unscathed. This is not a realistic definition of *recovery*. It just does not happen in real life.

If, on the other hand, *recovery* is to mean the outcome of healings from the impacts in the four dimensions of grief, and I accept I can only emerge as an altered person, in a forced altered life, having learned how to live with grief, probably for the rest of my life, this is a more realistic definition. It is what happens.

A parent is forever changed after experiencing the loss of their child.

There is no timeline for this kind of grieving. We can't hasten it.

We will grieve, in some form, forever, yet we can walk on with a graceful dignity and a sense of contentment.

20
Do Men Grieve Differently to Women?

The strongest person in the world is a grieving mother that wakes up and keeps going every morning.

Tara Watkins Anderson

My honest answer to this question is I do not truly know.

Every person's grief is unique to them, no matter their gender.

Each person's grief has its own home. No outsider can ever entirely enter that home.

A woman or man cannot know how they will react to grief until it crosses over their own doorstep.

A search of the literature reveals an abundance of articles and studies examining this question.

I did not find one report contending that men and women grieve the same.

I watched how Una grieved.

It was always painful to see her suffer so much in those early years.

No mother should have to suffer what I witnessed Una having to endure.

Do I know if she walked the same pathways as me?

Did she experience the same kind or degree of suffering and grief, as I did?

I don't know.

The best answer I can give is to be found in her book, *Ciara's Gift: Grief Edged with Gold*, a sometimes raw and transparent account of her pathways through her grief.

21
Impact of the Loss of a Child on a Marriage or Partnership

Grief knits two hearts in closer bonds than happiness ever can; and common sufferings are far stronger links than common joys.

Alphonse de Lamartine

Early statistics

Losing a child is never the norm; it has no point of reference.

When this happens to parents, their family changes, including their marriage. Grief will permeate their home, swathed in silence, for an unknown time, becoming a part of the air they breathe, its impact an unyielding physical force. They cannot act as if it has not happened and disown it.

The stakes are high.

Some couples may experience first the death of their child then the disintegration of their marriage or life together. I use the term 'marriage' to mean both a married couple and a couple in a de facto partnership.

The death of their child is a violation of the natural order of things. The subsequent grief is a complex process that follows no rules. Each parent's grief is wholly personal to them. No one can predict how they will react in such circumstances.

Years of a good marriage create layers of love, trust, selflessness, admiration, respect and reliance on each other. On the loss of a child, these layers are peeled back, revealing nerves that are raw, wounded and vulnerable.

When Ciara was murdered, every part of my grief screamed that I was alone, even though I had been married to Una for twenty-nine years.

In such circumstances how can parents prevent their marriage from deteriorating beyond repair?

In the early years following Ciara's funeral, I searched for as much information as I could find about overcoming what had happened to me as a parent and a husband, and to my marriage.

The most chilling sentence I read, by far, was: *Approximately 80–85% of marriages end in divorce after the loss of a child.*

I still remember reeling from that statistic. The more I searched and read, the more the number was confirmed. I had no way of checking its veracity, yet I could appreciate why this might be possible.

At the time of my early searching, the late 1990s, early 2000s, there was little empirical evidence to refute this scarily high number (at least that I could find). For perhaps two or three years I could not get the statistic out of my mind.

Around then, I made a private promise to do everything possible to prevent our marriage landing in that 80–85 per cent group. The frightening statistic had a value: it caused me to make that private promise and steeled me to find the determination to remain married.

It was nigh impossible to challenge the statistic at the time. Thankfully, since then other researchers have questioned its accuracy.

More recent statistics

Several later studies revealed there was no defensible evidence of such a high divorce rate, instead quoting figures of 15–30 per cent. A general difficulty in conducting this type of research is that the frequency of divorce in the Western world is reported to be about 50 per cent. Separating the actual contribution of the death of a child from other causes of marital breakdown in bereaved families is a problematic research question.

Stephanie Frogge in 'The myth of divorce following the death of a child' reports a wide-ranging review of research data on this topic. Her research concluded only two out of more than one hundred papers she reviewed found evidence of such high, i.e. the 80–85 per cent, divorce rates among parents who had lost a child.

There was no sure way of knowing if our marriage would survive despite the more welcomed lower statistics.

Irrespective of the accuracy of the statistics, parents dealing with the loss of their child will have an unbelievably tough and unpredictable road ahead of them, with no set timeline.

Still more recent research and reports

The internet is replete with websites dealing with the impacts of bereavement and grief on marriages. Many are scholarly articles on research undertaken within universities worldwide.

I visited much of this research, acquainting myself with its findings, as the quantity of publications increased.

The more recently published theoretical analyses of grief were not uplifting enough to continue searching for information on grief and marriage survivability. Understanding the subject matter, methodologies and sometimes complex statistical analyses reported in the studies was not foreign work for me.

A dominant focus of this more recent research incorporates information on what could go wrong within a marriage after the loss of a child. Other than generalities, few offered hope and direction on surviving and overcoming difficulties.

A great deal of the more recent material is the outcome of academic interpretations, gleaned from collections of individual stories, cases, descriptions or survey responses.

Such reports and studies may provide succour to some couples, even if it is only to affirm that what they are going through is not unique to them.

In the end, I decided if my marriage was to survive it would be up to me to chart my own course. If I did not sort things for myself, I would be little help to my family and to my marriage. I am not diminishing how difficult it may be for any person to make a similar decision. The temptation to surrender is not minor and is ever present, as is the attraction of just 'walking away from it all'.

Impact of early times of suffering on marriage

The early months and years for me are still a blur. At times I was catatonic with grief; my eyes were open, but I could barely function. I felt

I had been thrust into a world through which I had to blindly navigate my way.

Obviously, throughout a marriage couples change or are changed, but not so suddenly and in such distressing and stressful circumstances. It is axiomatic that all couples will alter, in different ways, shaped by how each responds to the shock and realisation of grief, and there is no certainty that their response tomorrow will be the same as today's.

There are no predictors of behaviour as to how a husband or wife will feel or deal with the early stages of profound grief. Even when grieving the same loss, wives, husbands and partners do not grieve in the same way. The published research says this is universally the case, irrespective of the length of time a couple has been together prior to the time of the loss.

At times, one person wishes for, indeed may need, silence whilst the other may need someone to confide in and perhaps to talk to about a particular aspect that is extraordinarily difficult for them. It is only occasionally these individual preferences seem to align.

To have an expectation the grieving by each will progress in the same cycles, or at the same pace, is unrealistic and inevitably leads to letdowns, setbacks and feelings of distance from each other.

There are times when one person simply wants to be, indeed *needs* to be, left alone. They do not want to hear about the other's feelings, they only wish to focus on their own. They only have the capacity to deal with their own grief.

At times like these, marriage can be both a blessing and a burden. It is a blessing not to have to deal with the grief alone, in an overall sense. It is a burden when it is all one spouse can do to survive, let alone help the other.

Avoiding discussion with or, more harshly, shutting out a spouse, especially in the early days, weeks, months and years, is often a self-protection mechanism. Unfortunately, I did not always recognise this as such at the time; this did not help.

Sometimes a spouse will not wish to speak about painful emotions and topics, and they wouldn't have to if they were grieving alone.

Expecting a partner to 'let it go and move on' when they are physically, psychologically, emotionally and spiritually doing their best to come to grips with what has devastated their own and both their lives is never helpful.

Yet, when married, in grief, and *desirous of staying together*, I believe each spouse, deep down, adopts a strong desire to cope with the suffering-filled memories. This includes discussing, even tentatively, very occasionally in my experience, individual perspectives on an unpredictable future. This is not easy to acknowledge or accept in times of new grief.

It is hard, for both.

A common belief is that partners have each other to 'lean on' and will be able to deal with the death of their child sooner and easier than other remaining family members. This belief is not true.

Couples don't just experience a cavity inside; they also have a cavity between them. In the early times of grief, they must cope with this latter, larger cavity that has opened up, over which they have little control, as it brings additional strains on their relationship.

It is no longer just the two together, yet at a distance from each other; there is the third, dark and sinister presence. It is called unasked for grief. The loss of a child can leave both partners feeling as if they are marooned on separate small islands of despair, though within sight of each other.

Overpowering grief, at least in the short term, can fracture either or both. It is understandable that each could justifiably feel there is nothing left inside, nothing left to give, even to their spouse.

I have mentioned to close friends that I lost Una to grief for over ten years. These years were the loneliest years of my entire life. Her return to the world was a most extraordinary experience to behold.

Marriages survive

It is a big ask to expect two people to work through grief at the same pace even when they have a shared loss. Grieving spouses can support each other but sporadically, as each tries to find pathways through their own, overwhelming sense of isolation.

Yet, if their wish to stay together is strong, they will do all they can to find a common pathway, or more likely individual pathways that seek the same destination. My experience is that whilst being tough, very tough, it was possible for us to do this, and I hope other parents find a way to do it, too.

Ciara was murdered in 1997. I am typing this twenty-five years later. Una and I have been married for fifty-four years, twenty-five of which are since Ciara's murder.

We survived.

We agree we emerged stronger, different people.

Marriages that have sustained the loss of a child experience the same valleys and peaks as any other marriage, except in a more devastating way. Whether the marriage becomes stronger or weaker, the one certainty is that the marriage will not be the same as it was before the child's death.

That is the norm and if both accept that, life together can continue.

Why and how did our marriage endure the loss of Ciara?

I don't know for certain. In no particular order, this is my best attempt at an answer:

> It was a choice I made, plain and simple, all those years ago. No matter what, I was going to remain strong and try my best to lead my family and remain married through what was to come, but not knowing how or if I would be able to do this.
>
> Through reading and searching I became knowledgeable about the possibility of a crash happening, at some time, that could annihilate our marriage.
>
> I accepted, without very much evidence, that men and women grieve differently and whether this is due to innate biological differences or other reasons is irrelevant.
>
> We allowed each other to grieve in our own way, in our own space, at our own pace; doing the best we could to honour each other's way of grieving; striving not to be critical of the other.

I learned, after some time, to not pretend I had dealt with my grief when I hadn't. I was not good at this. It hardly needs saying, men are not great at talking about this subject. I wasn't.

Not rushing into moving to a new house, in a new suburb, away from Ciara's 'home' helped – this was a correct call by Una; I wanted to move immediately.

Letting the grief find its own place in my altered life helped me.

I set out to foster a genuine trust in the unknown grieving process that would unfold, and as this happened, the grief would quieten and recede when the conditions were right, but never disappear from our marriage.

I took it one day at a time, not knowing what the future might hold, but trusting, praying, we would emerge, unquestionably changed, but intact as individuals, still married.

I learned to live with the pain-filled reminders of Ciara – birthdays, anniversaries, legacy events. These changed to less hurtful memories as time passed.

I sensed and believed both of us made an unspoken, internal commitment to do what we could to overcome the tragedy and remain together, though in the earlier years not knowing how to do this or if it was going to be possible.

The publication of Una's book revealed to me, for the first time, the extent and depth of her suffering and grief; this helped greatly.

I believe we tried to be there for each other, though at times this was severely tested by the enormous impacts of the unsought grief pervading our home, pervading each other, testing our marriage like nothing else.

I believe we have learned to live with our individual grief, accepting it is a part of who each of us is now, looking after each other, and being there for each other.

22
Use of Professional Grief Counselling

But grief is a walk alone. Others can be there and listen. But you will walk alone down your own path, at your own pace, with your sheared-off pain, your raw wounds, your denial, your anger, and bitter loss. You'll come to your own peace, hopefully....but it will be on your own.

Cathy Lamb

At the time of Ciara's murder, in 1997, there was a limited amount of publicly available literature on 'grief counselling', 'grief therapy' or 'grief support communities'.

Since then, there has been an explosion of published articles and studies on the subject as well as an enormous increase in the number of entities and communities offering grief counselling services, not to mention the hundreds of websites devoted to the topic.

Understandably, those offering grief counselling advocate use of their own or closely aligned services and are advocates of the benefits of these services. Much of the evidence for the claimed benefits I found to be in the form of personal 'life stories' drawn from clients/patients of the author or entity.

Even a cursory review of independent and academic studies on 'grief counselling' reveals divergent views on its efficacy.

In an article about online grief support communities, Hartig and Viola report:

> **individuals report less psychological distress because of joining these groups** – *and this psychosocial benefit increased over time. Individuals who were members for a year or more characterized their grief as less severe compared with those who had a shorter tenure in the community.*

Shishira Sreenivas in 'What is grief counseling?' states:

> **Psychologists, therapists, or grief counselors...can help you build resilience and coping strategies** *to deal with the intense sadness you may feel throughout your grieving process and help you find ways to move on in a meaningful way.*

Malcolm Winstanley-Cross in the online article 'Is counselling the best option to deal with grief and loss?' says:

> *What grief counselling offers are strategies to help you understand your own feelings and thoughts by increasing your clarity without feeling overwhelmed all the time...However, it is important to understand grief counselling is not a cure for the pain of bereavement.*

Hal Arkowitz and Scott Lilienfeld in their article 'Two big myths about grief' state:

> *when researchers have tested the common grief-work techniques of writing or talking about the death, some have found small benefits for the procedures, but* **most have not**. *In addition,* **the jury is still out on grief counselling**, *in which professionals or peers try to facilitate the working-through process...People are not always devastated by a death and should be allowed to* **recover in their own ways.**

One of the more comprehensive reviews of the question is 'What has become of grief counseling? An evaluation of the empirical foundations of the new pessimism' by Dale Larson and William Hoyt. This is a long read, best suited for those with an academic or professional interest in the topic.

I am cautious about readily accepting any view, either advocating or dismissing the use of professional grief counselling.

Counsellors do not have all the answers; no person does.

The use of professional grief counselling is *a very personal decision.*

I decided not to seek such help and instead continue, alone, to make the best sense I could of the altered world in which I found myself and from which I initially thought there was no release.

I found pathways leading to release, by unearthing a great deal of bloody-minded determination, doing hard work and trusting in the helpful and powerful forces within myself and those outside.

23
The Media and Grief

Grief is what we feel on the inside.
Mourning is what we reveal on the outside.
The media rarely pause to contemplate or come to know the difference.

Denis Glennon

Media coverage and its intrusion add to the trauma of parents who have lost a child. Parents can expect uninvited media involvement in circumstances where the police participate, a coronial inquiry is initiated or a regulatory agency investigates the matter when the loss of a child is due to natural causes, yet the local press wish to cover the matter for particular reasons. The intrusion is exceptionally acute and relentless in the case of a murder.

Media coverage, no matter the format – print, television, internet or social media – is hardly ever helpful to parents. In my case, its unsolicited presence predominantly brought only undesirable and unhelpful added pressures to already painful circumstances.

The dramatic headlines and subjective content cast unfounded criticism and doubt on the investigative work of police, on the work of scientists and investigators, all of whom were working diligently and conscientiously in search of the truth, seeking to find the person responsible for the Claremont Serial Killings.

The biggest surprise was the transparent insincerity of approaches to my family. Time after time we were requested to partake in stories, allegedly only emphasising the positive aspects of Ciara's life, how my family was impacted by the trauma, and how the reporter's particular content and tone in the published story would be of immense assistance to the police in their investigation. With a handful of exceptions over twenty-five years, the actual content or tone in the final publication never matched that promised.

Media coverage about police investigations, particularly of 'persons of interest', or on how my family and I were dealing with the loss of Ciara contained little more than selective information that supported the pre-disposed opinions of reporters, journalists and interviewers.

This reporting, particularly that prepared to meet nightly news deadlines, was habitually founded on deficient interpretations of the ever-increasing labyrinth of investigative information or on new 'evidence', allegedly gleaned 'exclusively' from 'reliable sources', most of which were hardly ever accurate.

On the occasions I declined to provide comment, the cruellest card of all was played: *If you don't agree to an interview or provide comment, we are going to run the story anyway, and you will have no chance to get your side of it across*. Unbelievable.

Even more cruel was the behaviour of a journalist representing an international newspaper. Within a day or so of Ciara's disappearance and during the time we did not know if she would be found, we received a late-night call seeking comment. My wife explained to the journalist that I had not informed my elderly parents, in Ireland, requesting him to give us time to contact them. His response: *I am going to run the story now, anyway*. I will never comprehend the callousness, insensitivity and egregious behaviour.

Such behaviour and reportage inflicted needless additional suffering on my family. The stomach-churning, sinking feeling that the early morning headline or the six o'clock news delivered was always beyond words.

This has been my lived experience, over a quarter of a century, and I am not alone in arriving at this conclusion on the media reporting of the Claremont Serial Killings.

Ciara's disappearance, the discovery of her body, early details of the homicide, the police investigation over two decades, the lengthy trial, the uniqueness of the case and the conviction and sentencing of Edwards – each aspect generated its own groundswell of media pursuit and intrusion. There was no avoiding this onslaught, right up to the end of the trial and, for a brief time, immediately following.

Such coverage has both instant and long-lasting effects, dredging up painful memories, invading privacy, lifting hope, killing hope and prolonging trauma. The countless re-running of video footage of the locations where Ciara was thought to be abducted and where her body was found, along with the search, by some media, for negative information on her from friends, as if she somehow contributed to her disappearance, created never-to-be-forgotten stress and trauma for my family.

I had had no previous direct contact with, or experience in dealing with, forceful media approaches. The aggressiveness of local, national and international media came as a shock to me.

The barrage of requests for comments, photos of Ciara, interviews and countless other invasions of privacy were confronting and overwhelming. We changed our telephone number at least four times, only to have our privacy breached repeatedly. Over time, I learned to deal with it.

It was necessary to remain hopeful and stay strong, to shield my family as much as I could.

The impacts on us, specifically around the uncertainty of how long the police investigation might take, were mercilessly intensified by tactless, speculative media coverage. The more aggressive, younger reporters believed they possessed an inherent right to have their questions about Ciara, my family and me answered immediately, frequently as they followed me up the street with a microphone in my face. Some older, experienced reporters were more considerate and understanding.

When questions were respectfully declined and answers were not provided, the media wilfully speculated on the work of the police and scientists involved in the investigation, or how they thought my family or I was dealing with things, knowing full well they were working with limited or unsubstantiated information, and, on a small number of occasions, information that could only have been in the public arena because of leaks from inside the police force.

In the long run, such leaks, and the publication of same, served no good purpose and did not influence in any positive way the successful outcome of the investigation.

My personal experience includes journalists and photographers waiting for hours at the entrance to our home; persistent ringing of the doorbell; calling my mobile and home phones; emailing; texting; dogged requests for input to an article or television news piece going to air in 'the next few hours'; requests to provide comments for books and articles being written; requests to partake in television documentaries in the making; requests to share the raw grief being experienced; and offers of payment to participate in documentaries.

These requests were falsely founded on baseless claims: *it is in the public interest; the public have a right to know*; or *it will be cathartic for you to speak about it*. All fallacies.

Such requests and subsequent media reports served little or no legitimate public interest value or purpose.

Irish philosopher and poet John O'Donohue was correct when he wrote: *The media is essentially like Plato's Cave – a parade of shadows that we take for the real world. It is a huge abstraction from what is real.*

Suspicion and scepticism do not have to be the prime currency of dealings between media personnel and those seeking truth and justice, especially in times of grief.

Journalistic standards and editorial stewardship which tap the deeper wellsprings of the long-established principles of impartiality and empathy are indisputably superior alternatives, but which sadly are in decline. I listened to but a small number of the daily podcasts during the trial. They consisted of little more than personal commentary and speculation by those participating, no depth, and commonly no respect for privacy.

There were several professionals in the media whose ethical standards I found to be unquestionable and who, with acumen and wisdom, crafted balanced reports which were sensitively worded, transparent and honest.

Dealing with these professionals was best handled in one-on-one interviews where the impact of questions could be observed by the interviewer and considered as the discussion progressed, as well as reaching agreement that the contents of the interview would not be published until I was comfortable with the content and particularly the tone of the 'overall message' conveyed, whilst still respecting editorial prerogatives. Such reporting and consideration were always a welcome respite.

Always, at the forefront of my mind, was the protection of my family and care for my own wellbeing. Also critical was finding constructive ways to interact with media personnel so that they would continue to be somewhat less critical of the investigative efforts whilst remaining at a respectful distance, and to forestall or avert the more forceful reporters from dominating the agenda.

Over time, I learned to:

> be honest
>
> never lie
>
> be friendly, courteous and respectful, especially when asked questions on family and personal matters, acknowledging the media had 'a job to do'
>
> try to be composed, as much as possible
>
> deal with journalists and interviewers in a calm manner, showing respect to those attending
>
> not speculate on outcomes of investigative work undertaken by police or others
>
> politely refuse to answer spontaneous questions seeking my opinion on the work of the police or others involved in the investigation
>
> prepare brief notes and advise the media present I would speak from the notes

offer to get the information to journalists as soon as I could in response to legitimate questions for which I genuinely had no answer at the time (and I did)

be aware the interview started as soon as I commenced speaking, even if a camera, microphone, mobile phone or notebook was not in sight

assume all dealings with the media would be 'on the record' even when told the interview would be 'off record' or I had 'proof of copy'

not speak on behalf of anyone except my family

never to reply 'no comment'; instead provide an answer such as 'I can't reveal that information now'

be careful of what I said to other people when media were close by, believing whatever a journalist hears can be and will be reported if it suits their or, more likely, their editor's purposes.

The WA Police helped, at the conclusion of the trial, in arranging two media conferences, to which all media were invited and for which I had the opportunity to prepare comments I wished to make as well as general responses to anticipated questions.

These 'guideposts,' in the later years, engendered a mutual respect and contributed to the partial extent of privacy afforded us at crucial and tough times, especially during the long ninety-five-day trial.

Since my final public statement, on 24 December 2020, the media have overall respected my request for privacy for my family, and for which I thank them.

24
The Trial and Resurrection of the Impacts of Grief

If one set out by design to devise a system for provoking intrusive post-traumatic symptoms, one could not do better than a court of law.

Judith Lewis Herman

Our justice system represents the community response to a crime. It provides a very public acknowledgement of the crime and offers an opportunity for justice. My family will be eternally grateful to the criminal justice system that delivered a verdict and appropriate sentencing of the person proven to be responsible for murdering Ciara. However, understanding and navigating the complexity of the legal system, which at first appears to be cumbersome and drawn out, is not easy.

No matter the time between the loss of a child and the eventual trial of the perpetrator, the physical, emotional and psychological impacts of grief may return with a vengeance during criminal proceedings, in the time between the verdict and the outcome (sentencing), and at the sentencing itself. The outcome frequently remains unknown until the final minutes of the sentencing hearing.

It is not possible to predict if the impacts of grief will return or how upsetting they will be if they re-emerge. The three months between the verdict being announced and the sentencing I found to be particularly tough.

Having been through the physically, psychologically and emotionally draining long trial, where every day was understandably pre-scheduled by the judicial system, the end of the trial was welcomed. The prospective date of sentencing was set for three months later.

In the vacuum suddenly created, my mind instantly switched to the unknowingness of the sentence and the possibility of an appeal.

Sleep was elusive, long hours spent churning through unsolvable scenarios.

How many years imprisonment would the sentence impose?

What would be the minimum parole period? Would he ever be released to hurt, rape and kill other young women?

If an appeal was mounted what would this mean in terms of the timing and length of a new trial?

Knowing the collateral damage I experienced by then, would I remain as closely involved, if the sentence was appealed? If I didn't, how would I deal psychologically with that?

What impact would an appeal, if mounted, have on members of my family and on my own health? How would I deal with the inevitable, heightened media frenzy, no matter the sentence?

How would I deal with the reported screening of two documentaries by Australian television, if they came to fruition, in the next year or so?

Irrespective of the actual sentence, what kind of lasting detrimental impact would Ciara's murder have on my family? Would some form of post-traumatic stress disorder (PTSD), which to date had well and truly been absent, raise its unwelcome head?

It was the unknowingness of the above in the environment of the understandable silence of the judicial system, I found so tough. Too many times the unanswerable questions and concerns ate into my soul.

The most immediate question was, should my family prepare one or more victim impact statements?

In Australia, family members of murder victims may speak in open court, at the hearing that decides the killer's sentence, about the effects of the murder on their lives. This is known as a 'victim impact statement'. Judges may take into account the impact of the crime on the family in passing sentence, but may also disregard any opinion the family expresses about the perpetrator or about the sentence they believe should be passed. It is a voluntary process, designed not to influence the sentence imposed but to give family members the opportunity to express their grief in open court, rather than perhaps to the media on the court steps afterwards. The preparation and writing of a statement is a very traumatising experience as it inevitably causes you to 'relive' the entire suffering and grief.

The decision to attend a trial is a personal one, as is the decision to provide a victim impact statement.

I chose to attend the trial but not provide a victim impact statement.

The trial lasted ninety-five days. It was a prolonged and painful experience, as I attended practically every day. The only days I did not attend were those when the medical details of the autopsy on Ciara's body were presented and argued. Graphic photography and videos of the autopsy were seen only by the judge and members of the legal teams representing the prosecutor and the accused. I followed the advice of the lead prosecutor and did not attend during those presentations and discussions.

Images that are seen can never be unseen.

During the lengthy trial, I listened to and viewed testimony on the circumstances of Ciara's disappearance, the unsuccessful struggle between her and her murderer, the discovery of her body concealed by vegetation, the horrific details of her fatal injuries, the arrest of the accused, his initial denial of any involvement, his surprise admission to additional non-fatal attacks on two other women, his verdict and sentencing.

Many times I struggled to understand how the court system appeared to be more protective of the rights of the accused than those of the person murdered and their family. As the trial progressed, I developed a better understanding of the balance a judge must maintain throughout the proceedings. Siting in the same room as the accused, for approximately five hours per day, my emotions varied from an initial intense anger towards him, being appalled at his constant expressionless, unremorseful discard and denial, to a huge sense of relief when the sentence was delivered.

I was left speechless by the accused's barrister's arguments apropos the possibilities of the dominant DNA evidence being contaminated in the laboratory where it was stored in an unopened container for over twenty years, as well as his arguments about the origin of the fibres found in Ciara's hair and on her clothes. Both the DNA (found under Ciara's fingernails because of her struggle to save herself) and the fibres from a motor vehicle's carpet and upholstery were crucial pieces of evidence that led to the accused being found guilty and sentenced to life imprisonment.

The entire court attendance was, every day, a revisiting of the earlier grief I experienced.

The physical impacts were again felt as I had to push myself to get out of bed, shower, dress and travel to the courtroom, every morning. The temptation to not attend was strong.

The psychological impacts resurfaced as I tried to understand and had no choice but to accept the glacial pace of the hearing. I was but a bystander, with no opportunity to do or say anything; the same as any other 'left behind' family member.

The emotional impacts returned the strongest of all – *sadness, anger, resentment* towards the accused, *fear* of the outcome, at times a *loss of trust* in the justice system, *despair* when the case seemed to be proceeding in favour of the accused, *helplessness* at not being able to contribute a single thing towards the outcome I dearly sought.

The spiritual impacts hovered around but were never really tested to the extent of the other three.

Not knowing how the trial would end, many times I was doubtful if the healings and manifestations I had worked so hard to find, over many years, would remain intact and I would otherwise be catapulted back to the early times of grief, reverting to the vulnerable, wounded person I was then.

In retrospect, the trial was a three-month assault on how I had come to terms with my grief; if I had truly learned to live with it and if the healings could be depended upon to see me through to the end. They did.

Had I not been in a place of contentment with my grief, it would have been impossible to attend the trial. No setbacks were experienced. I grew stronger for being present.

Victim impact statements are optional and voluntary.

I did not prepare one. I trusted the judge and the justice system.

Had I prepared a statement, its presentation would involve me speaking directly to the accused, laying out intimate details of his savagery when he killed my daughter, and how, over a period of twenty-five years, his brutality impacted and changed my family and me.

There was no honourable reason to go through the pain of reliving or restating this.

I formed the view that Ciara's dignity would have been debased by sharing such private details in the very public environment of a courtroom, or with a person who had not shown one morsel of remorse during the entire trial.

He had done enough damage to my family.

25
In the Public Spotlight

It always seems impossible until it's done.

Nelson Mandela

Una's book, *Ciara's Gift: Grief Edged with Gold*, written over a ten-year period, was published in 2012. In it, she described her grief at losing Ciara:

> *Days that are meant to be days of celebration are now days tinged with sadness.*
>
> *There is always someone missing, a conspicuous absence, an empty chair…her silence speaks louder than our words. We miss her acutely.*

The words will forever resonate with me, with imperishable clarity and meaning.

When Ciara was deemed a missing person, in 1997, in a television press conference, appealing for help to find her, I said: *She would fight for her life. Because of the way she's been brought up, she will fight.*

Little did I know how prophetic these words would be.

Twenty-plus years later, scientists investigating her murder unearthed the vital DNA clues that were keystone evidence leading to the conviction of Edwards. Ciara fought to save her life.

Ciara was strong in spirit and had courage. Yet she could not save herself from the brutal assault.

I was advised not to view Ciara's body. I read the complete autopsy report shortly after it was compiled. The autopsy report contained the photographs of the fatal injuries to her neck and body. The same images were disclosed at the lengthy trial but were unseen by the public. They were too confronting. For over two decades I continued to live with these images. They are indelible.

Shortly after my *fear a'tidgh* experience, outlined in chapter 12, I visited Ciara's grave, alone, remaining on the periphery; it is a hallowed place, sacred lawn. My commitment made to Ciara on that visit, that I would do all in my power to find the person(s) who murdered her, drove me unwaveringly, unapologetically and, on many occasions, very publicly, for over twenty years.

This occasioned continuous interaction with members of the police force and others over nearly a quarter of a century: meetings with detectives, officers in charge of the investigation, coroner's office personnel, external investigative specialists providing advice to the police, several case reviewers, people in the community who believed they might be able to contribute, a range of 'disturbed' persons claiming to have information identifying the murderer, clairvoyants – some well-meaning, a wide range of people external to the police claiming 'special' expertise, people writing books, many media personnel, prosecution lawyers and so on.

During the investigation, spanning twenty-three years, there were several lines of investigation which provided little or no advancement, all frustrating and disappointing for everyone. In times likes these it appeared as if the investigation was making little to no headway. Each of these setbacks generated cascades of negative media commentary on the alleged lack of expertise of scientists and insufficient efforts by the police to solve the killings. To remain resolute, retain confidence in the police and scientists, tested my deepest values, confidence and belief that justice would prevail.

I have no criticism on what the police and scientists might have done differently during the lengthy investigation. I have no critique of those involved. These people did the very best they could with the information, methods and equipment available to them at the time of their involvement, and all of which became superior as new techniques were developed over time.

Nothing revealed in the trial came as a surprise to me, including the honest mistakes made along the way, several of which could only be discovered because of advancements in DNA technology, nearly two decades later.

The Western Australian Police Force permitted me to enter their world and express my profound desire for justice. They were honest and open, always. I met with a member of the police force, on average, every month, over twenty-five years. They allowed me to assist wherever they believed I could. My request for truthfulness of information, no matter how hard to hear and bear, was granted.

We trusted each other. This trust and level of confidentiality will forever be honoured, never be forgotten.

My requests to meet, seek clarification and try new investigative techniques, and offers of assistance to unblock impediments in the search for the murderer were never refused. No reasonable request was declined, no sensible suggestion was devalued.

Despite the long period of time, a termination of the investigation by the police force was not seriously considered at any time, especially when breakthroughs were heartbreakingly elusive. Nor was termination a preferred option when lines of enquiry, frequently running over many months, proved futile, despite valiant efforts by dedicated professionals to bring the investigators closer to identifying the killer.

The extensive investigation would not have continued over such a prolonged period without the allocation of appropriate resources, and the personal interest and support from various Commissioners, Deputy Commissioners and Assistant Commissioners, some more than others, and senior officers. The momentum may have waned on occasion, but it never stalled.

To those devoted people who were there when it mattered, on behalf of my family, I thank you, sincerely. You know who you are.

More than five hundred police officers, over twenty years, were involved in the investigation and in the three years of rigorous preparation for the trial following the arrest of the accused.

Scientists, profilers, case reviewers and specialists in New Zealand, the United Kingdom, the United States of America and elsewhere conducted many meticulous reviews and much analytical endeavour. I came to know most of them.

The police force's willingness to break with orthodoxy and explore new avenues for clues helped establish groundbreaking investigative practices in Australia, some of which, in the early years, were funded by colleagues in the Perth business community.

It was the commitment, openness and rock-solid endeavours of the police force and scientists that sustained me during the times of setbacks. I never doubted their ability and commitment to find Ciara's murderer.

The Office of the Director of Public Prosecutions for Western Australia's chief prosecutor and her team also took my family into their confidence, as they did with the other families impacted by the Claremont Serial Killings. I witnessed the insightful, penetrating, unremitting pre-trial assessment of evidence and the indefatigable advocacy during the ninety-five-day, judge-only trial. No amount of personal exhaustion impeded their efforts – all remarkable professional women, with very big hearts.

Circumferential to all this were the constant requests and demands from media for commentary on the status of the investigation, in particular my views on 'dead ends' and 'persons of interest' that arose throughout.

Traversing the public minefield in which I found myself was new for me. It was the path I chose, to assist and insist on finding the person who murdered Ciara. I have no regrets about that choice. Ciara would expect no different of me.

As best as it can be in this world, justice has been delivered for Ciara.

My family and I are where we are for many reasons. The most notable is, unquestionably, the faithful and steadfast support we received from the West Australian community, over so many years, for which there are not enough words to capture its significance and meaning to us.

We will be forever grateful for their presence in our lives during those difficult times.

26
Contentment – What Is It?

Until you make peace with who you are, you'll never be content with what you have.

Doris Mortman

The word *contentment* derives from the Latin word *contentus*, meaning 'contain', 'held together', 'be intact', 'be whole'.

My view of a *contented* person is: *a person who is intact, feels complete, with no desires to be in a different position to where they are.*

My life is acceptable, exactly as it is, right now.

I am content.

If circumstances change from time to time, I trust in myself to find more pathways to discern these changes. I will not spend time speculating what changes might arrive. Trust will continue to be my greatest friend, to cross any new thresholds that time throws up.

I will not be a prisoner of the past.

The perpetuation of this state of *contentment* requires input from the inside and is open to input from the outside, including from the soul or spiritual side.

Whatever I need to maintain *contentment*, nourish it, I turn to inward reflection, and to the outside, to Una, to my family, to selected pieces of writing, music, to nature, to my soul, to my spirit, to God.

All are plentiful with caring.

Contentment, despite all its apparent ephemerality, is not something somebody gave to me.

It is one of the outcomes from Ciara's murder.

I am at home with my sadness as I am with feelings of my *contentment*.

Thoughts and feelings come and go; there is no necessity to try to change them or judge them.

Contentment is the brother, the sister, of the Japanese wabi-sabi philosophy and the creative art of Kintsugi.

In simple terms, my *contentment* is one of ease with my situation, in body and mind, in heart and spirit, at ease with the idea that the knowledge I have of my grief is enough.

I feel at home in my heart, and at my home's hearth.

27
A View from the Ridge

It is not the mountain we conquer, but ourselves.

Sir Edmund Hillary

Morris West's last book, *A View from the Ridge,* is not so much a novel as an autobiography. From it, I borrow three quotes, which seem apt for this last chapter:

> *We have to admit, first to ourselves, and then, very humbly, to one another, that we live at the heart of a dark mystery, which* **we can still only describe by allegory and legend or the sterile and incomplete formulae of physical science.**
>
> **One has to accept pain as a condition of existence. One has to court doubt and darkness as the cost of knowing. One needs a will stubborn in conflict,** *but apt always to the total acceptance of every consequence of living and dying.*
>
> *If God be God and man a creature made in image of the divine intelligence, his* **noblest function is the search for truth**.

With acknowledgement to Morris West, I have titled this last chapter, *A View from the Ridge*, that is, a retrospective view.

Healing from the impacts in the four dimensions of grief doesn't mean I will never again fall back into sadness. It means I will be able to have good and bad memories without an attachment to the despair of grief.

The healing of the impacts of the four dimensions brought a harmonious blend of mental toughness, restored strength, determination, courage, wisdom, truth, enlightenment, comfort, peace and contentment.

Moments of peace, from my marriage to Una, love for Ciara, and Denise and our four grandchildren, appreciation of life, happiness, fond memories, calmness and goodness come at unexpected times, in serendipitous ways. These are enough to convince me the insights and manifestations I experienced along the way are worthy of trust, and will stand me in good stead, to the end.

These insights and manifestations will endure and I will continue to turn towards them, even if my sadness and loneliness still, on occasions, go unrelieved for a while.

They have helped transform tragedy into strength and resilience.

They have stood the test of time. They are authentic and worthy of trust.

Suffering can potentially be integrated by every parent, in their own way, at their own tempo. Healing can be experienced in the deepest of suffering. Paradoxically, it can be grasped in moments of darkness, of abandonment of hope, and of apparent helplessness. To the 'why' of suffering there is no answer. Yet it is in those moments we make a critical choice, to acknowledge we need to seek guidance, assistance and healings from sources outside our fractured selves, and be grateful for their serendipitous arrival when they come. They fortify our internal strengths.

The alternative is to fall into the suffering and grief, collapsing into our own human smallness at just the time when that smallness can no longer contain the deadening weight of our grief.

The resolve to take steps to rebuild our lives, aided and strengthened by manifestations along the way, can deliver a better understanding of the place of grief in our altered life.

The enlightenment about God's presence in it all was a revelation of significance, giving added meaning to the universal human condition, assisting me to clamber over the highest hurdle.

To find a genuine space of contentment, all four dimensions of grief needed to be explored, exposed to personal, sometimes painful enquiry, to find pathways towards healing their impacts.

The four dimensions are inextricably interconnected, symbiotic, as are their impacts.

It is difficult for me to comprehend how parents can find the insights, the determination and courage to come to grips with the deep tragedy of losing their child, to find the indomitable strength in the human spirit, without being touched by the invisible, mysterious presence of forces within themselves, and by outside forces, larger than themselves.

Yet many must, and do, find ways of overcoming their grief, without being touched.

Others never do and do not find meanings, or release from, their tragedy.

Please be easy on such people.

We cannot ever know their suffering, the unremitting weight of their grief, but we can listen reverentially.

If I trust to continue to follow the pathway I am on, life, loneliness, contentment will continue to be made more serene, more sacred, more peaceful, making my grief more habitable, my soul re-experiencing the geography of its destiny.

The proof of that is, even though I have been through hell, the most profound grief still has not blunted or destroyed the essence of who I am.

Changed, yes; destroyed, no.

There is no denying my family and I have been impacted, on many fronts, but we have also experienced healing.

Una and I are still together, our marriage still strong.

There, I find increasing love, peace, contentment.

Grieving never ends but it need not end life.

The past was unquestionably engulfed by sadness, but is transcended by fond memories of Ciara, watered by tears, but caressed by her spirit, her courage. These memories will continue to apply healing balm to my grief.

I have been able to step beyond the assaults of grief and experience a joy in life that is entirely new to me.

I am at peace with the circumstances in which I find myself.

I did not always see it that way.

I am accommodating my grief; it is an integrated part of me.

Ciara would expect no different from me.

Life's shadows are lengthening for me now.

From here, thankful for the mysteriously restored strength, courage and enlightenment I received, I move forward with composure, renewed purpose and meaning, shepherded by fond memories from the past, melded with the future, with Una, our remaining daughter, Denise, our four grandchildren, with friends, and with thoughts of enduring gratitude to so many people.

As best as it can be in this world, justice has been delivered for Ciara.

I discovered deep within grief how to appreciate beauty in imperfection, walk on with equanimity, solace, appreciation and public grace, never to forget or stop loving my beloved daughter Ciara.

Alongside Una and Denise, I keep her close, always.

I am one of the fortunate ones.

Bibliography

Academic articles

Albuquerque, S., Pereira, M. and Narciso, I. 'Couple's relationship after the death of a child: a systematic review', *Journal of Child and Family Studies, vol. 25,* no. 1, 2016, pp. 30–53, https://doi.org/10.1007/s10826-015-0219-2.

Hartig, J. and Viola, J., 'Online grief support communities: therapeutic benefits of membership', *OMEGA – Journal of Death and Dying*, vol. 73, no. 1, 2015, https://doi.org/10.1177/003022281557.

Larson, Dale G., and William T. Hoyt, 'What has become of grief counseling? An evaluation of the empirical foundations of the new pessimism', *Professional Psychology: Research and Practice*, vol. 38, no. 4, 2007, pp. 347–355, https://doi.org/10.1037/0735-7028.38.4.347.

Oliver, L.E., 'Effects of a child's death on the marital relationship', *OMEGA – Journal of Death and Dying*, vol. 39, no. 3, 1999, https://doi.org/10.2190/1L3J-42VC-BE4H-L.

Rogers, C.H., F.J. Floyd, M.M. Seltzer, J. Greenberg and J. Hong, 'Long-term effects of the death of a child on parents' adjustment in midlife', vol. 22, no. 2, 2010, pp. 203–211, <http://doi.org/10.1037/0893-3200.22.2.203>.

Schoenberg, Debra, 'How the death of a child can impact a marriage', *Family Therapy Magazine*, July/August 2020, pp. 36–38, <https://www.sflg.com/wp-content/uploads/2020/07/Debra-Schoenberg-JA20.FTM-1.pdf>.

Books

Bennett, Enoch Arnold, *Sacred and Profane Love*, 1905.

Brown, Elizabeth, *Surviving the Loss of a Child: Support for Grieving Parents*, Revell, Grand Rapids, MI, 2010.

Camus, Albert, *The Sea Close By*, Penguin Books, 1954.

Carmody, Mitch, *Letters To My Son: Turning Loss To Legacy*, Beaver's Pond Press, Edina, MN, 2011.

Cholbi, Michael, *Grief – A Philosophical Guide*, Princeton University Press, NJ, 2021.

Devine, Megan, *It's OK that You're not OK: Meeting Grief and Loss in a Culture that Doesn't Understand*, Sounds True, Boulder, CO, 2017.

Farley, Kelly, with David DiCola, *Grieving Dads: To the Brink and Back*, Grieving Dads, Aurora, IL, 2012.

Frankl, Viktor E., *Man's Search for Meaning*, Penguin Random House, Sydney, 1959.

Greenspan, Miriam, *Healing Through the Dark Emotions: The Wisdom of Grief, Fear, and Despair*, Shambhala Publications, Boston, 2003.

Herman, Judith L., *Trauma and Recovery: The Aftermath of Violence – From Domestic Abuse to Political Terror*, Basic Books, New York, 1992.

Kalsched, Donald, *Trauma and the Soul: A Psycho-spiritual Approach to Human Development and its Interruption*, Routledge, 2013.

Kelly, Jill, *Peace in the Face of Loss*, Tyndale House Publishers, 2017.

Kempton, Beth, *Wabi Sabi: Japanese Wisdom for a Perfectly Imperfect Life*, Piatkus, London, 2018.

Kemske, Bonnie, *Kintsugi: The Poetic Mend*, Herbert Press, 2021.

Koren, Leonard, *Wabi-Sabi for Artists, Designers, Poets and Philosophers*, Imperfect Publishing, 2008.

Kushner, Harold, *When Bad Things Happen to Good People*, Schocken Books, New York, 1981.

Lewis, C.S., *The Problem of Pain*, The Centenary Press, 1940.

McCarter, Melissa Miles, *Joy, Interrupted – An Anthology on Motherhood and Loss*, Fat Daddy's Farm, 2013.

Nietzsche, Friedrich., *The Nietzsche Anthology*, Bybliotech, 2014.

O'Donohue, John, *Anam Cara: Spiritual Wisdom from the Celtic World*, Penguin Books, Sydney, 1998.

O'Donohue, John, *Walking in Wonder: Eternal Wisdom for a Modern World*, Convergent Books, 2018.

Pausch, Randy, *The Last Lecture*, Hachette Australia, Sydney, 2008.

Powell, Richard R., *Wabi Sabi Simple: Create Beauty, Value Imperfection, Live Deeply*, Adams Media Corporation, 2005.

Roe, Gary, *Shattered: Surviving the Loss of a Child*, Healing Resources Publishing, Wellborn, TX, 2017.

Roland, David, *The Power of Suffering: Growing through Life Crises*, Simon & Schuster, Sydney, 2020.

Rosenblatt, P.C., *Help Your Marriage Survive the Death of a Child*, Temple University Press, Philadelphia, 2000.

Seidman, Mark, *Grieving Dad: Surviving and Healing the Loss of Your Child*, CreateSpace, 2016.

Spungen, Deborah, *Homicide: The Hidden Victims*, Sage Publications, Thousand Oaks, CA, 1998.

Thich Nhat Hanh, *No Death No Fear: Comforting Wisdom for Life*, Riverhead Books, 2003.

Thomas, Claude Anshin, *Hell's Gate*, Shambhala Publications, Boston, 2006.

Thomas, Claude Anshin, *Bringing Meditation to Life: 108 Teachings on the Path of Zen Practice*, Oakwood Publishing, Florida, 2021.

Valters Paintner, Christine, *Eyes of the Heart: Photography as a Christian Contemplative Practice*, Sorin Books, Notre Dame, IN, 2013.

Valters Paintner, Christine, *Earth – Our Original Monastery*, Sorin Books, Notre Dame, IN, 2020.

Weinberg, Steven, *Dreams of a Final Theory*, Vintage, Reading, 1994.

West, Morris, *A View from the Ridge: The Testimony of a Twentieth-century Christian*, Harper, San Francisco, 1996.

Wolterstorff, Nicholas, *Lament for a Son*, William B. Eerdmans Publishing Co., Grand Rapids, MI, 1987.

Young, Julian, *Friedrich Nietzsche: A Philosophical Biography*, Cambridge University Press, New York, 2010.

Films

Alive Inside: A Story of Music and Memory, directed by Michael Rossato-Bennett, 2014.

The Gifts of Grief, directed by Nancee Sobonya, 2005.

Websites and blogs

Arkowitz, Hal, and Scott Lilienfeld, 'Two big myths about grief', *Scientific American*, 1 November 2011, <https://www.scientificamerican.com/article/grief-without-tears/>.

Cave, Nick, *The Red Hand Files*, <https://www.theredhandfiles.com/>.

The Center for Prolonged Grief, Columbia University, <https://prolongedgrief.columbia.edu/>.

Collier, Graham, 'Music: one of our most profound creative achievements', *Psychology Today*, 6 October 2016, <https://www.psychologytoday.com/us/blog/the-consciousness-question/201610/music-one-our-most-profound-creative-achievements>.

Cordaro, Daniel, 'What if you pursued contentment rather than happiness?', *Greater Good Magazine*, 27 May 2020, <https://greatergood.berkeley.edu/article/item/what_if_you_pursued_contentment_rather_than_happiness#When:10:40:00Z>.

Dolan, Yvonne, 'What is solution-focused therapy', Institute for Solution-Focused Therapy, *HealthyPsych*, <https://healthypsych.com/what-is-solution-focused-therapy-by-yvonne-dolan-ma/>.

Frogge, Stephanie, 'The myth of divorce following the death of a child', *TAPS*, 1 March 2015, <https://www.taps.org/articles/21-1/divorce>.

Glennon, Denis, 'Solitude and sea part 4: solitude and night sky', *Sail World*, 13 November 2006, <www.sail-world.com/28737>.

Good Therapy, 'Coping with grief: why forgiveness matters so much' by Wendy Salazar, 23 May 2014, <https://www.goodtherapy.org/blog/coping-with-grief-why-forgiveness-matters-so-much-0523144>.

Harvard Health Publishing, 'The power of forgiveness', 12 February 2021, <https://www.health.harvard.edu/mind-and-mood/the-power-of-forgiveness>.

John Hopkins Medicine, 'Forgiveness: your health depends on it', <https://www.hopkinsmedicine.org/health/wellness-and-prevention/forgiveness-your-health-depends-on-it>.

Lloyd, George, 'What is "wabi sabi"?', *Japan Today*, 4 August 2021, <https://japantoday.com/category/features/opinions/what-is-wabi-sabi>.

Metz-Allan, Nola, 'The impact of forgiveness on healing and grief', *The Mighty*, 20 August 2021, <https://themighty.com/topic/grief/letting-go-of-guilt-healing-from-grief/>.

Moutzouris, Ivette, 'What happens when we forgive', *The Resilience Centre*, 26 August 2016, <https://www.theresiliencecentre.com.au/2016/08/26/what-happens-when-we-forgive/>.

PammyV02, 'Nietzsche on the power of music', *Photography & Vision*, 30 November 2015, <https://photographyandvision.com/2015/11/30/nietzsche-on-the-power-of-music/>.

Richman-Abdou, Kelly, 'Kintsugi: the centuries-old art of repairing broken pottery with gold', *My Modern Met*, 5 March 2022, <https://mymodernmet.com/kintsugi-kintsukuroi/>.

Schurman-Kauflin, Deborah, 'Why you don't always have to forgive', *Psychology Today*, 21 August 2012, <https://www.psychologytoday.com/us/blog/disturbed/201208/why-you-dont-always-have-forgive>.

Sreenivas, Shishira, 'What is grief counseling?', *WebMD*, 3 August 2021, <https://www.webmd.com/balance/grief-counseling>.

Thomas, Samira, 'In praise of patience', *Aeon*, 12 May 2016, <https://aeon.co/essays/how-patience-can-be-a-better-balm-for-trauma-than-resilience>.

Tippett, Krista, 'Meditation seventy-three: beauty is our calling. God is beauty (interview with John O'Donohue)', *The Spirit of Life*, 18 June 2020, <https://www.spiritoflifecommunity.org/liturgy/pastors-letter/236-meditation-seventy-three-beauty-is-our-calling-god-is-beauty-interview-with-john-o-donohue-6-18-2020>.

Trites, Elizabeth, 'Music: mediator between the spiritual and sensual', *Music 345: Music and Religion*, 19 September 2016, <https://pages.stolaf.edu/musicandreligion/2016/09/19/music-mediator-between-the-spiritual-and-sensual/>.

Winstanley-Cross, Malcolm, 'Is counselling the best option to deal with grief and loss?' *Counselling in Melbourne*, 4 May 2018, <https://www.counsellinginmelbourne.com.au/is-counselling-the-best-option-to-deal-with-grief-and-loss/>.

About Upswell

Upswell Publishing was established in 2021 by Terri-ann White as a not-for-profit press. A perceived gap in the market for distinctive literary works in fiction, poetry and narrative non-fiction was the motivation. In her years as a bookseller, writer and then publisher, Terri-ann has maintained a watch on literary books and the way they insinuate themselves into a cultural space and are then located within our literary and cultural inheritance. She is interested in making books to last: books with the potential to still be noticed, and noted, after decades and thus be ripe to influence new literary histories.

About this typeface

Book designer Becky Chilcott chose Foundry Origin not only as a strong, carefully considered, and dependable typeface, but also to honour her late friend and mentor, type designer Freda Sack, who oversaw the project. Designed by Freda's long-standing colleague, Stuart de Rozario, much like Upswell Publishing, Foundry Origin was created out of the desire to say something new.